The Family Self-Help Book

Exercises in Family Synthesis

DEBORAH SMITH ONKEN, PH.D.

FAMILY SYNTHESIS INSTITUTE®
ST. LOUIS, MISSOURI

Printed in the United States of America
First Edition

For more information, contact Family Synthesis Institute, P.O. Box 9439, St. Louis, MO 63117, USA.

ISBN 978-0-9799868-2-6

Cover and logo design by Sheldon Helfman

This book is dedicated to

*all the couples, families, individuals,
and students who have taught me so much about purpose,
potential, change, and resilience in spite of the challenges they faced.*

ACKNOWLEDGEMENTS

I discovered Psychosynthesis in 1975 at a conference for counselors. By the next summer I had started my Psychosynthesis training in Edmonds, Washington, at Ed Turner and Doug Russell's training institute, Highpoint Northwest.

I returned there for several summers, and then started working under John Parks, M.D., director of The Kentucky Center of Psychosynthesis in Lexington. Both Parks and Turner had worked with and been trained by Dr. Roberto Assagioli in Italy. Edith Stauffer and Tom Yeomans also trained with Assagioli and were guides for me.

Through Parks I met and learned from Mark Horowitz, Lenore Lefer, and Molly Young Brown, as well as many others. But probably one of my closest guides was Vivian King, a psychologist who trained in Psychosynthesis under Stauffer. King and I trained other professionals in Psychosynthesis for six years before she died. I am also deeply indebted to Mary Kelso, another psychologist and Psychosynthesis trainer, who specializes in working with children and families, and helped develop and research the Family Synthesis Questionnaire with me.

Finally, my heartfelt thanks to those who read my first draft and made suggestions to improve it:

- Judith Broadus, psychologist and trainer at the Kentucky Center,
- Dale Kuhn, director of Care and Counseling, a pastoral counseling institute in St. Louis,
- Linda Strominger, a Methodist minister in St. Louis,
- and most of all my deepest thanks to Susan C. Thomson, my editor and friend.

St. Louis, Mo.
November 2007

INTRODUCTION

You can find books and web sites today to help you fix just about anything in your life—your house, your car, your yard, your appliances, even your relationships. Most of the writers assume that these things are broken or painful. This is a self-help book for families, but it is not about brokenness and fixing it. It's about discovering and building on the positive, the good, the strength, that already exists in every family.

This book encourages you to discover your family's essence through coming to know better not only the family you live in now, but also the influences of the generations that have come before. In the process of discovery, you will examine all your family's behaviors, good and bad, and become more aware of the choices you are making.

By drawing on the functional aspects in our families—their constant, deep, and unique identities—we can better live through the inevitable crises and changes of life and come out more whole. The authentic identity of each family, re-expressed over the generations by each new marriage and family unit, diversifies and enriches society and reflects the multiplicity of mankind and all creation.

Psychiatrist Murray Bowen has observed that families hand down through the generations ways of dealing with trauma and change. Some of these ways are useful, helping us get through problems successfully and feeling strengthened. Other inherited patterns such as anxieties, addictions, suicides, abuses, and depressions so mire us in dysfunction and fear that we deny or run away from our problems rather than face them. As a result, most of today's therapies and therapists are concerned with helping families identify and cope with their dysfunctions. Too few look at the positive aspects of a family's inheritance and its potential for growth.

Yet, when a family faces its problems knowing its potentials as well as its dysfunctions, even though afraid, it will discover its purpose and meaning in life. It is in finding a family's purpose that it gains the resilience and the strength needed to deal with life's inevitable setbacks and changes. As family therapist Monica McGoldrick says, "All families should be assessed for their resilience as well as their problems."

Such thinking parallels that of Dr. Roberto Assagioli (1888-1974), an Italian psychiatrist who saw potential and purpose in each individual and society. In his theory, called Psychosynthesis, he described individuals, groups, and societies as whole organisms with levels of consciousness and unconsciousness. He said that consciousness at any one moment for any group or individual included perceptions and combinations of memories from the past, awareness of the present, and possibilities for the future. His psychological theory is part of a body of theories called Transpersonal Psychology or, more recently, Positive Psychology. Like Assagioli, these psychologies state that we are physical, emotional, thinking, and spiritual beings.

This book draws heavily on Assagioli and his understanding that we have innate strengths, even while pain is disrupting our life. He emphasized that in order to grasp our whole personality, find our purpose, and realize our inherent potential, we must learn to "disidentify" from the habitual defenses and perceptions he called subpersonalities and "re-identify" with who we really are, our true Self. He said we can't change by identifying with pain and stuck behavior but can change only by stepping back and finding our center.

Only from this center, which Assagioli calls the "conscious self," or "I", can we make choices about our behavior that are consistent with our purpose, meaning, and possibilities. The conscious self is a mirror, a spark, and a projection of the Higher Self. These two selves are one whole that is experienced in different degrees of awareness. In this book, to make the spiritual Self more apparent to the family, the family will first seek understanding who they are and their family self, their "I", knowing that it is the conscious projection of Self and of Truth and Love.

While Assagioli did not apply his theory to families, he saw them as having the same problems and potentials as individuals. Family Synthesis, as used in this book, combines Assagioli's theory and versions of his exercises with family systems theory, which sees the family as an inter-related unit where each member has a role or subpersonality determined by the family's interactions.

I have developed Family Synthesis over a thirty-year career as a psychologist, counseling individuals, couples, and families as well as conducting Psychosynthesis training and workshops, teaching university undergraduate and graduate students, and lecturing in the United States and abroad.

Family Synthesis, a positive psychology, sees each family as having a center, or family self, a purpose, and all the strengths, endurance, and resilience that have been passed down through the generations. Each marriage provides an opportunity to express the family purpose in new and creative ways. A family that can recognize its transmitted possibilities is better able to handle the stressors of life, support each other, and give members more choices for fulfilling their own purpose and the family purpose.

Family Synthesis theory holds that each child carries a unique configuration of genes from each parent and each parent's family and is born with gifts, blessings, and potentials ready to be expressed. Jungian analyst James Hillman affirms this concept and adds that the body, parents, place, and circumstances of our birth are a choice of our soul and its purpose or call. Therefore, recognizing that we have a call and aligning our life with what he calls our "original soul pattern" allows us to express our reason for being.

So, immediately after birth, babies start to adjust to their surroundings and "join" the families they will live in. This happens in families of all configurations, including traditional, blended, single-parent, and those with same-sex parents. Out of love and self-preservation, the children take on their family's culture, understandings, and values. They even take on their parents' bad habits and perceptions about themselves so that the parents can accept their own failures and be able to love themselves.

When children grow up and marry, they carry on the tradition by imitating their parents' marriage. This does not mean that they marry a mother or father clone, but rather that they unconsciously imitate their parents' interactions, with all their mistakes and possibilities. Their unconscious hope is to uncover the inherent goodness and potential of generations of marriage and act them out more creatively and effectively over a lifetime.

The following story illustrates this pattern. It is the first of many in this book; names and personal characteristics have been changed to protect identities.

SUE'S STORY

Sue came into therapy anxious, depressed, and beaten down. Her first husband had died and left her with two small children. She worked hard to support her family and some years later met Joe, who wined and dined her and doted on her children, so she eventually married him. Almost immediately after the wedding, he started verbally abusing her and putting her down. She stayed in the marriage, thinking she could eventually "get it right" and he would become the man she thought she married.

When her children were in high school and college, she decided she wanted to complete her own college degree in order to get a job to help the family income. When she asked Joe about this, he said, "NO, you aren't able to do college work. You are only fit for menial work. Stay home and wash the floors." He added, "If you go back to college, I'll get a divorce." In a few weeks he showed up at the house with divorce papers and said he would file them if she ever tried to go back to college. It was at that point that she sought therapy.

During the therapy, she told her family's story, beginning with her grandmother. In the 1890s Sarah met, fell in love with, and married Sam. He deeply loved and admired her, her strength, and her independent spirit. When she wanted to work for women's rights and become a suffragist, he supported her but told her, "Just be home in time to fix me dinner and take care of our children." Her fellow marchers teased her about getting home by five to make sure dinner was ready on time, but she felt this was her compromise and her support of Sam.

One of her daughters, Beth, heard her father's injunction and decided that her mother was too independent. When she married, she rarely left her home and was very dependent on her husband. By the third generation, Beth's daughter

Sue had married her abusive husband, Joe, who kept her at home with a very meager amount of money for the household, clothes, and support of the children.

When her oldest child, Liz, was ready to go to college, Sue found something stirring in her. She wished she could just stay home, be dependent like her mother, and obey her husband. She had not stood up for herself before, so why was there now a push inside her to go to school and be independent? During counseling she began to recognize her abilities and creativity and remember stories of her grandmother's strength and independence. She eventually went back to college and is working in a job she loves and where she can be effective.

She also began expressing herself more clearly in her marriage. One day she discovered pictures of her husband with another woman, another wife several states away. Joe and Sue are now divorced.

In the meantime, Liz, of the fourth generation, met Rob in college and they decided to marry. Sue quickly recognized that Rob sometimes talked to Liz in a demeaning manner, and she worried that their marriage would repeat a dysfunctional family pattern. Liz told her mother that she planned to get her degree before they married and that she and Rob would get counseling. Liz said, "I want to marry a man who can be my best friend so that we can love and respect each other's independence in the world."

Some people may want to read this book straight through, while others will want to take one chapter at a time in order to discuss and experience each exercise more thoroughly before moving on to the next. Still others may do only one, two, or three of the exercises. Some of the exercises will promote laughter, story telling, and enjoyment, while others will bring forth deep discussions. No matter how you use the book, the exercises will take you on a journey of family discovery that will go on for many years.

Many of the exercises are written as scripts, which designated family members, serving as leaders, can either read aloud or record in advance. Leaders can be family members taking turns with different exercises. Leaders may also be therapists or other professionals working with families or small groups as clients. It is helpful to have the leader read the exercise in advance and, when reading the script to the family, do it reasonably slowly to give people a chance to think about what is being said. A pause at the end of each paragraph also helps participants think or write about what they have just experienced.

The rest of this book presents theory and techniques all families can use to realize and express, or live out their inherent multi-generational potential. The book's exercises are to help family begin their journey into the growth and purpose in their family relationships.

For most of the exercises family members will need pencils, paper, or art materials. I recommend "journaling," or writing down or drawing insights and thoughts, so that participants can see, read, and remember what the exercises have taught them about their family. This is also a way to ground or make real the experience of the exercise.

It is important that all immediate family members participate together and that everyone is clear about their choice and intention to be with the family for this time. Make sure the place where you sit, stand, write, or draw is comfortable, and all phones are on answer or put away.

A note on capitalization: This book follows Assagioli's custom of capitalizing words like Self and Purpose when he uses them to denote the spiritual, Holy, or God.

EXERCISE: BREATHING AND CENTERING

Before beginning any exercise, it is important to "center." This means to quiet, let go of distracting thoughts and emotions, and become present to the group and the exercise.

A common centering practice focuses on breathing.

LEADER:

"Get comfortable in your chair, with your feet on the floor and your back fairly straight but not rigid. Close your eyes and start focusing on your breathing. As you breathe, let go of distracting thoughts and emotions and keep bringing your mind back to your breathing. Be aware that as you breathe in, you are breathing in life-giving oxygen, and as you breathe out, you are letting go of any impurities in your body. Breathe in goodness, and expel any worries or concerns.

"As you continue breathing, realize that you are feeling more alert and, at the same time, more relaxed. Focus on your body's relaxation and see if there is one area that seems more relaxed than the rest of your body. Focus on this area, allowing a color to come from it, like a cloud or vapor.

"Allow your color to start expanding to nearby areas of your body and relaxing them. Allow the color to go up and down your spine and relax your stomach. Now move the color up to your head, and let it relax your thoughts as you breathe in and out. Your thoughts become more present and focused on your breathing and the color that is washing over them.

"Slowly but surely, allow the color to keep expanding until your whole body is wrapped in this relaxing and protective color.

"Your breathing has relaxed you yet has made you more present, more aware of the environment around you. Now realize that your color represents relaxation.

"With all of the exercises in this book start by breathing deeply and wrapping yourself in your color for centering, relaxation, and readiness. Your color helps you maintain a boundary between your body, thoughts, and feelings and others around you. Your insightful mind allows you to experience each exercise and share what you are comfortable sharing. If you are uncomfortable in any exercise, center, breathe, wrap your color around you, and listen."

CHAPTER 1

FAMILY SYNTHESIS AND RESILIENCE

Life today is stressful, fast-paced, and anxiety-producing. It is filled with the risks of losing love, friendship, employment, health, money, and security. We often feel powerless in the face of events beyond our control. The results are evident. Depression and drug and alcohol abuse are common. Suicide rates are up, especially among teens.

In our increasingly nomadic society, relatives live at greater distances from one another, and family relationships seem more tenuous and fleeting than ever. Couples live together and produce children without marrying. Divorce is an accepted way of life, resulting in more and more children living in single-parent households and spending weekends in different homes.

Yet our ancestors also had to live through wars, loss of parents, poor health, and many other obstacles we can't even comprehend. Like them, we need to find that well of resilience and survival in each of us. Resilience is the ability to adapt, bounce back, and remain competent and confident in the face of crisis. Without this behavioral flexibility, we are unable to deal with setbacks. With it, we can buffer ourselves from the worst effects of our negative experiences and even learn from them.

Mental health practitioners today are becoming more interested in investigating and describing ways that seem to help people stay healthy, survive change, regain equilibrium, adapt, and go on after hardship, crisis, and even catastrophe. Resilience isn't just survival. It is, as family therapist and researcher Froma Walsh describes in her book *Strengthening Family Resilience*, "an active process of self-righting and growth." Resilient individuals may experience disruptions in their normal functioning, but across time they are able to function healthily and consistently with their personality. They grieve. They fully experience trauma and loss but are not shattered by them. They are able to cope.

MARY'S STORY

Mary had heart disease with multiple angioplasties and stents. On vacation, far from home, her chest pain became so pronounced she had to get to an emergency room fast. In the hospital, doctors told her she would need bypass surgery. Her heart was functioning so poorly that she would not survive the trip home. Four days later, with the pain increasing again, she was told that she would be operated on the next morning, or even that night.

As night approached, she started praying for the strength to survive. She worried about leaving an ailing husband and mother. She sang old hymns to herself and slept sporadically. Suddenly she remembered being five years old with her family on a vacation. They were staying at the home of a distant relative and it was night. The three children had been fed and put to bed upstairs, while the parents and others had a late dinner party downstairs.

Mary's younger brother woke her to say he had to "go potty." This also woke her younger sister, so all three crept down the hall to the bathroom. Coming out of the bathroom was a woman guest, who so frightened the children that they ran down the stairs screaming, "Mommy-Daddy, Mommy-Daddy, Mommy-Daddy," and into their parents' arms at the dinner table. Kindly, they were taken back to the bathroom, back to bed, and comforted.

In her hospital room, Mary imagined all her family back with her, comforting and strengthening her through the night. The next day the surgical staff was amazed at her calm and strength as she started into surgery. No one knew if she would survive the surgery, but she knew she was back in the arms of her family, and their love, strength, purpose, and structure were with her. She did survive and could tell the story of how she knew her family could work together to survive any situation. Although all of Mary's grandparents and her father had died, her mother was in a wheelchair, and her brother and sister were married with families and living far away, all were there that night with Mary.

The American Psychological Association is campaigning to help individuals and groups understand what resilience is and know that they can learn it. Among the factors APA ascribes to resilient people are self-confidence, communication, problem-solving skills, and the ability to make and carry out realistic plans. To build resilience, the APA says, we must have important connections with others, accept crisis and change as parts of living, set goals according to a purpose, and work toward them. Equally important are maintaining hope, searching for self-discovery, nurturing a positive view of ourselves, and focusing on the long term.

The flexible outlook and self-worth that are so important to resilience can be learned in and supported by interactions in the family. This book sees the family as a place to learn and develop resilience in the family and in each member. Through discovery of the family's potentials and purpose and the attitudes that help it handle trauma and change, each member of the family gains a stronger sense of connection and confidence. These inner resources can often get lost when the family needs them the most, but family stories, traditions, and models help us remember them.

MY STORY

When I was young, my father told me this story of his great-grandmother and her daughter who lived in a log cabin on the frontier.

The two women were alone in the loft of the cabin making soap with hot lye and ashes while the men of the family were out hunting. Both women heard a noise outside and looked through the small upstairs window to see a group of marauders approaching the cabin door. The women sensed that the marauders knew there were no men around, and they feared that they could be raped, murdered, or captured.

Quickly Great-Grandmother told her daughter to help her take the caldron of hot lye to the upstairs window, which was over the front door. When the marauders were all standing at the front door, both women poured the hot lye down on them. The marauders ran away screaming and did not return. The women's quick thinking and courage had saved themselves and their home.

I cannot tell you how many times I have remembered this story when I felt overwhelmed by my concerns. I knew I had in me the courage to act and find a way that would save my family and me in any situation. Thank you, ancestors, for your example of strength and intelligence in adversity.

In an article called "Loss, Trauma, and Human Resilience" (2004), psychologist George Bonanno, known for his work on bereavement, identifies four pathways to resilience: hardiness, self-enhancement, regressive coping, and positive emotion and laughter:

1. ***Hardiness*** includes having a sense of purpose in life, and a belief that we can influence events and learn and grow from them.

2. ***Self-enhancement*** is the sense of well-being that helps us cope positively in dangerous situations.

3. ***Regressive coping*** is the ability to put emotional responses aside, while not denying them, in order to function in an emergency. Widows with small children often tell about functioning for the children and then crying in their beds at night. We will return to this idea when we explore Assagioli's technique of "disidentification."

4. ***Positive emotion*** and laughter can reduce distress and increase the likelihood of contact with and support from others. Adults and children who can laugh and smile in spite of their pain have better chances of adjusting after it.

DOROTHY AND MARION'S STORY

As only children and only first cousins of each other, Dorothy and Marion were closer than most sisters. Within months of each other, Dorothy married John and Marion married James, and the pairs became couple friends, drawn to one another, in part, by similar senses of humor.

The four stayed good friends through Marion and James' divorce and became a threesome after Marion died of ovarian cancer and then another foursome when James married Ruth.

John's diagnosis of terminal lung cancer was a blow to all. "What can I do to help?" James asked Dorothy, John's wife. "Make me laugh, just as you have always done," she answered. And so, over more than a year of John's fruitless chemotherapy and radiation, James, from 1,000 miles away, kept in close touch with Dorothy by email and phone, offering a joke or funny comment whenever he could. Without him, Dorothy says, she couldn't have gotten through John's illness and death. Even through the worst, James' humor, love, and wisdom were always with her.

Martin Seligman, founder of Positive Psychology, coined the term "learned optimism," and wrote a book by that title (1990). He says that optimism can be taught and that a family with an "optimistic bias" is more resilient in the face of change. The opposite is "learned helplessness," which Seligman describes as a hopelessness caused by experiences of defeat and lack of control and choice.

Seligman says our parents, teachers, peers, and even life itself can teach us how to handle criticisms and failures. If we see our failures as opportunities to learn and as calls for action, choice, and growth, we can build hope and optimism in our children and ourselves. We can empower our families to know their creativity and capabilities.

Froma Walsh's work with resilience underscores Bonnano and Seligman's point that the family that finds meaning in adversity and sees crisis as a shared challenge often has a belief system that is the "heart and soul" of its resilience. This belief system usually relies on family stories, family heroes and, as role models, older family members. Families that have this, while accepting what cannot be changed, have a positive view, sustain hope, and focus on strengths and potentials. They believe in the values and purpose of the family and each member. Walsh also emphasizes the importance of faith, rituals, and openness to new possibilities and service to others.

Without acknowledging Assagioli, the American Psychological Association, Bonnano, Seligman, Walsh, and other positive psychologists recommend what Assagioli wrote about in his *Manual of Psychosynthesis* in 1965, years before any of their publications. In his book, he also talked about purpose, disidentification, self-enhancement and identity, growth, humor, and laughter. He developed exercises to help individuals look for meaning and purpose so that they could live fruitful lives and learn from change.

From understanding his theory and doing the exercises in this book, families can realize that, like the individuals that make them up, families themselves have positive potentials and purposes that seek as much expression as do old negative patterns of behavior. For the family, as for individuals, fearing and resisting their purposes and potentials, instead of acknowledging and working with them, can be just as psychically painful as reliving old traumas.

In the following chapters, your family will talk about the exercises, look back over generations, and start to see how your ancestors struggled to survive, had an identity, and found meaning in the world and creative ways to express their potentials and purpose. Remember, each family has a unique, generations-old identity and a drive for expression in the world.

Families pass on this identity through the stories they tell of heroes, families, and events. Each new marriage and child brings with it potentials for expression of the family identity. Sometimes this expression is frustrated, discouraging families and even tearing them apart. This does not have to happen. Through searching for each person's and each family's purpose, laughter, and soul, all families can change and grow.

To find its unique potential, purpose, and self, the family must start to explore who they are now and who they have been. In the following chapters, we take this step by step, starting with an assessment of family traditions, qualities, and strengths. Next we help the family make choices that will build hardiness and resilience. The family does this by mobilizing its will and recognizing its true self, or unifying center. When the family discovers its true self, it can join around this center and experience its purpose. Finally, the family can heal past hurts and resentments through forgiveness, gratitude, dreams, and joy and move on to express all its meaning to the world.

EXERCISE: FAMILY PURPOSE

This exercise is similar to one Psychosynthesis author Piero Ferrucci has used with individuals, and is designed to help a family clarify its purpose. As with many of the exercises that follow in this book, family members need to have pen and paper handy for "journaling," or making notes about their experiences. Some family members, especially the children, may also want to have drawing materials to record their experiences visually.

Set aside a time when everyone can be together, free of distraction, in a comfortable place, and remind the leader to pause after each paragraph so people can reflect and write.

LEADER:

"As you quiet, focus your mind on your choice to be here today and choose to be open to the family and the exercise. Now think of what you see as this family's main purposes. Jot them down now. There are no right or wrong answers. Some may be hard, others easy to realize. Some may be lofty and distant, others specific and immediate. All that matters is that they are important for you and the family. *[Pause]*

"Choose one of the purposes on your list that seems most important to you now. Close your eyes and let an image emerge that symbolizes this family purpose for you. This image could be anything from an abstract symbol to an animal, an object of nature, a person, a word, or a sound.

"With your eyes closed, imagine a long straight path in front of you going directly to the top of a hill. On top of the hill see your image symbolizing the family purpose.

[Go slowly in the next section.]

"In your imagination, start walking up the path with your family. See, hear, and feel the presence of various influences, human and other, trying to divert the family from its path and keep it from reaching the top of the hill. They will do anything they can, including discouraging you, frightening you, making you feel guilty, and telling you how stupid or absurd you are, but they cannot block your family's path, which remains straight and clear.

"Keep deliberately walking, even as these entities talk and jeer at you. When you reach the top with your family, see the image of your purpose waiting for you. Talk to it and listen to the wisdom it has for you and your family. See the sunlight bright overhead shining on your image, you, and your family, strengthening your sense of purpose. Thank the light and your image for being here with all of you.

"Gradually open your eyes and write down what you have seen, heard, and learned from persevering on the path up the hill and being at the top."

After everyone has had time to journal or draw their experience, quietly share with each other what purpose and image you discovered for the family on the path.

You can repeat the exercise at any time, taking other purposes that you first jotted down, finding their image, and taking the path up the hill to them. Each time be aware of choosing to stay on the path even when other thoughts, feelings, and physical experiences want to pull you away. Although the purpose is important, so is the journey to it.

CHAPTER 2

THE FAMILY MEETING

A family meeting is one of the best places to start finding resilience in the family. Some families have weekly meetings, if only informally at the dining room table. The meetings that are the basis of the exercises in this book should be relaxed but not casual and have a structure with ground rules.

To make the discussion and exercises most effective, set aside a time and place, checking with each family member to make sure it is as convenient as possible for the group. This lets all know how important they are. Choose a setting with as few distractions as possible. Put all phones, including cell phones, on answer. Turn off the TV and radio. Use comfortable chairs.

Should everyone be included? Does that mean the baby? Not necessarily, but by the time children are three, four, or five years old, they know who the family is and are very much part of it. They may not understand everything, but they have their own wisdom and can add to any discussion. Yes, the older children will be able to discuss more and enter in better, but participating in a family meeting is good for everyone.

Who should be the leader? The parents may want to lead the first few meetings, but the leadership should change so that each person has a chance to set the agenda and take charge. If the family is using an exercise, the leader needs to read it earlier and bring the necessary supplies.

How often should a family meet? Some families set aside an hour a week or every other week; others do shorter times and more often. The meeting should not be a burden but an opportunity. Each meeting should have time for sharing and an opportunity for solving any problems that come up between meetings. When a family first starts doing meetings, exercises such as those that follow help build comfort, which can be helpful when hard problems need to be discussed.

A family meeting usually starts with each person sharing something that was important from the past week. In order to make the sharing safe for each person, boundaries, both physical and emotional, need to be recognized. People differ in their reactions to being touched or how close they sit with each other. Some show feelings and share ideas and opinions freely. Others fear hurting someone, being judged, telling a secret, or disagreeing. Respect the choices of those who want to share only a certain amount or nothing at all. Realize the family unit also has a boundary, and so decide what the family is willing to share with others, including extended family and friends, and what it wants to keep confidential.

It helps the family to have some specific techniques for starting the sharing. Tom Yeomans, a Psychosynthesis author and trainer, leads groups that have a leader and also share the leadership with all members. Three of his most important rules are to practice presence with each other, allow silence, and be nonjudgmental of all members, welcoming and even seeking out differences. All three of these principles can be applied to family meetings as well.

1. ***Presence*** means not only staying in the moment with other family members but also focusing your attention on them and what they are saying. It means listening with your whole self to their whole selves—their creativity, pain, or wisdom. It means listening to what has happened, is happening, and could happen for the speaker. Presence also means showing empathy, or willingness to experience what the speaker is trying to communicate, putting your own responses aside, and being with the other person in every way you can—physically, emotionally, and mentally.

2. In our noisy society we are often uncomfortable when there is ***silence*** in a conversation, and we jump in to fill the void. Yes, silence can be negative, a way of not sharing our anger, sadness, and fear. However, there is also the silence that allows us the freedom to share and truth to speak to us. For three hundred years the Quakers have known that sitting in Silence and welcoming the Holy, or Truth, benefits each person and builds a community.

The family is a community of its own, and in the set-aside time of the family meeting, being silent and waiting for each person to speak can be supportive of the less vocal members. Psychosynthesis therapists often start their client sessions with meditation, simply breathing, being quiet, and focusing on their intention and the purpose of a meeting. In Family Synthesis I do the same and start family meetings with a period of quiet before anyone speaks.

3. A ***nonjudgmental*** attitude on the part of all participants fosters better sharing. In an atmosphere of presence and nonjudgment, where only one person speaks at a time, family members who are reluctant to share may find it safe to talk. This same atmosphere, which allows people to share vulnerability, welcome differences among themselves, and talk about what they are observing in the family, helps the excessive talkers as well. In most cases, as the family builds trust, it will settle down and allow others to share.

Froma Walsh talks about "mutual empathy" in a family, which results from being tolerant of individual differences, taking responsibility for one's own feelings, avoiding blaming, expressing emotions openly, and having pleasurable interactions, including humorous ones.

She also stresses that it is vital for family members to give and listen for clear, consistent messages. In times of crisis and change, fear can alter an individual's perceptions of a situation, so it is important for family members to communicate, share emotions, and understand each other. Crisis experiences are more manageable when family members share information and openly discuss the meanings and implications of events.

A good way for family members to clarify communication is a technique called mirroring, described by psychologist Harville Hendrix in his book on marriage therapy, *Getting the Love you Want.* He describes a communication exercise in which people are "senders" or "receivers." A sender says something he or she would like the other person or family to hear. The "receiver" puts aside any feelings or pre-existing answers to hear the "sender," not to agree, just to listen to what is being said and repeat it back later.

Before the family meeting, there might be an exchange like this:

> **SENDER:** "I don't want to be here tonight because I have other plans."
>
> **RECEIVER:** "I heard you say that you do not want to be here tonight because you had previous plans. Did I get that right? Is there more you would like to say about this?"
>
> **SENDER:** "Yes, I was not asked when to set this family meeting, and I don't like changing my plans and missing my (friends, TV, soccer, work, ___________)."
>
> **RECEIVER:** "I hear that you resent not being asked about the time of this meeting and are upset. You feel your plans were not considered and you don't like being pressured into this meeting. Is there any more?"
>
> **SENDER:** "No."
>
> **RECEIVER:** "I would like to respond now.______________."

In this kind of listening, the receiver does not respond or try to solve the situation but lets the sender experience being heard. In turn, the sender becomes the receiver, responding with the same listening skills the other person used. Receivers may worry that they sound as if they are parroting and not helping the sender, but senders feel empowered when they are heard. By taking the risk of telling someone something personal, the sender builds self-esteem and success.

After opening the family meeting with a few minutes of silence or centering to get everyone's whole attention, ask each person to tell something good another family member did in the past week. Then ask each person to tell the family something good he or she did in the past week. Encourage family members to give examples of what they did to solve problems and to show their strengths and abilities. Doing this at the beginning of the meeting allows time for all members to become accustomed to sharing something positive about themselves and others.

In one of these earlier meetings, set aside time to do the following exercise, which is designed to help the family look at who they are now as well as who they have been in the past. Have plenty of paper, journals, and art supplies on hand. If not before this exercise, then soon after, find a box, for storing the products of this and future exercises. This box needs to be large enough to also store special pictures, objects, and papers that have meaning for the family and that the family can collect in order to share its heritage with the generations to come.

EXERCISE: WHAT KIND OF AN ANIMAL AM I?

This exercise is based on a common children's game. Many families use it to help children know the different animals and to mime the animals' behavior. If you have young children and have never done this exercise, you might take the time before the meeting to list many different animals and briefly describe them and their behaviors.

For this exercise you need slips of paper and pencils, pens, or crayons. Give each person as many slips of paper as there are members of the family. Ask each person to write their name on one slip of paper and one family member's name on each of the other slips of paper. Young children who cannot write yet could use a crayon to draw family members' pictures on their slips. For this beginning exercise, you might want a parent or older child to be the leader.

LEADER:

"Now that everyone is seated and has their slips of paper, become quiet and think of all sorts of different animals. Take a slip of paper with someone's name on it and write down the name of an animal that is most like that person. You might say that someone is a bear, a dog, a tiger, a deer, a cat, or a fish. Whatever animal you first think of for that person, write it down.

"Now do the same with everyone else in the family. On the slip of paper with your name, write the animal you think you are most like."

After everyone has finished writing or drawing, ask each person to get up in turn and hand to each family member their slip of paper with the animal's name on it. Take a few minutes for everyone to silently read their slips of paper. Then take turns reading your slips of paper aloud and explaining, if possible, why you chose a particular animal for a particular person. For example:

- "Dad is like a Dalmatian dog because he would protect us in a fire."
- "Mom is like a cat because she is clean and playful."
- "Susie is like a puppy because she is fun."
- "Dan is like a snake because he knows how to crawl on the ground."
- "Sam is like an elephant because he is big and can walk long distances."

If some of the answers are negative, help the family member also realize the positive aspects of this animal. Point out to the tiger of the family, for instance, that besides being fearsome, that animal is a great hunter and very protective of its family. Continue after everyone has shared.

LEADER, *continuing:*

"Now choose which animal you will be for the next week. Choose it for yourself and not because you are afraid of being criticized or of upsetting the other family members. Whatever animal you choose will be right since you are going to explore this animal for a week and can do another one in another week. Put the animal's name on a slip of paper and keep it with you all week.

"Stand up and experience this animal in your body. You may tell each other what animal you are or decide to let each other guess. Stretch and even make sounds like this animal. Walk around the room like your animal and meet the other animals in the room. See how you interact with each other. Do you want to hurt each other? Stay away from each other? Play with each other? Do you have respect for each other? What do you do with each other? *[Pause to walk around]*

"Go back to your seat, take out your paper and try to answer these questions. *[Pause often for writing]*

"What is there about this new animal that seems to be like you? What qualities does this animal have? How do these qualities work in the family and out in the world? How do they help the animal adapt?

"**Purpose:** What purpose does your animal have in this family and in the world of animals? Why is it important to all other plants and animals on Earth and its ecology?

"**Adaptation:** How has your animal adapted to its environment, climate, and ecology? How does this animal communicate with other animals in its own species and why? How does it solve its problems? How does it interact with other animals for its survival? How has it adapted over many generations?

"**Resilience:** Has your animal shown resilience to changes in its habitat? Consider animals such as deer and coyote that we now have in our suburbs. Has your animal survived over many thousands of years, like turtles, fishes, lizards, and insects?

"**Family Life:** What is the family life of your animal like? Does this animal survive in families or packs or is it a loner? Are you the male of female of this animal? Note the different lifestyles of the sexes and what, if anything, they contribute to the rearing of the young." *[Pause for everyone to finish writing or drawing about their animal.]*

"During the week, notice the other animals in the family. How does this family of animals get along? How does it live in the same house? How does one animal influence the other animals in the house? If you have a tiger and a rabbit in the house, how does the rabbit keep from being eaten? Does it hide in its room? Also notice how your animal acts with people outside the family—at school or work, for instance. If possible, keep a brief journal of your animal observations during the week."

At the next meeting ask all family members to share how their animals interacted in the house and outside the house.

LEADER, *at the next meeting:*

"What did each of you learn about yourself and others? What did you learn about the family?

"What is there about the second animal that you would like to be more like? How would this second animal interact with others in the house, school, or work? What is the purpose of this new animal in the family?"

As the family looks at the animals with each other, they are also looking at the roles they play with each other and how they influence each other in their choices. Before the family completely leaves this exercise, ask each other about which of the family's animals are resilient, able to adapt and survive:

- Can this whole family of animals do the same?
- What qualities will this family need in order to adapt and survive?
- How has this family adapted and survived over generations?
- What is the purpose of this family over all of those generations?

This same exercise can be done with flowers, plants, colors, cars, machines, heroes, or movie or book characters. The purpose is to free up the everyday perceptions we have of each other and to look at our roles in the family and society and at the family as a whole and its special identity in the world. No matter what the family composition is, whether it is multigenerational or fractured by divorce, it still can look at its reasons to survive or to die off. If there have been breakups, divorce, or no surviving children, then who is left and what do they want to express to society?

Don't forget to store your answers and drawings in your box. The next chapter will give you even more chances to get to know your family better and add more to your box.

CHAPTER 3

FAMILY MEMORIES

Ethnic and cultural values strongly affect the family patterns that repeat themselves over generations and are reflected in our attitudes toward roles, age, birth order, individuality, and communication. We can observe this through our genograms, timelines, family trees, and the Family Synthesis Questionnaire.

Genograms are elaborate family trees showing family interaction patterns through the generations. Like family trees, they show births, marriages, and deaths. They also show medical histories, family roles, occupations, major life events, and how family members interacted with each other. For information on how to do them, see Appendix III.

A timeline, popularized by psychotherapist Ira Progoff, who used it with journaling, visually captures personal and family events in chronological order, looking at our development, potentials, and how we grow and come to reveal and understand who we are. He looks at what he calls the "steppingstones of life" and what connects the generations. The family can also make a timeline, using each person's individual timeline to build a family timeline and see the family steppingstones.

The questionnaire, based on one by Assagioli, and updated for the family by Mary Kelso and myself, explores the multigenerational transmission of the family's culture and ethnicity. These two exercises will help you organize your family history. They can be stored in the family box that you set up in the previous chapter, along with the earlier exercises and other memorabilia.

You can start with either the timeline or the questionnaire. Children and adolescents often find a timeline intriguing. If you have a collection of family stories, traditions, and culture, you may want to start with the questionnaire. Begin where your family is more interested.

The exercises bring new understanding of the family and may raise more questions. Although most family members may agree on basic information, their different perceptions may color their descriptions of incidents or relationships. Accepting each person's contribution without judgment is important.

These exercises can be done in a family meeting, or they can be done individually and brought to one or more family meetings for discussion. For both exercises, you might want to interview extended family members for their knowledge of family history.

EXERCISE: FAMILY TIMELINE

First, each family member creates an individual timeline. Start with colored pencils, markers, crayons, and a roll of white shelf paper. Cut off enough paper for each person to draw a line representing his or her life from birth to the present time, and then extend that line ten to twenty years into the future. Depending on their age, family members may want to divide their lines into five- or ten-year segments.

LEADER:

"On your line, note each important happening in your life, including births, deaths, marriages, divorces, and moves. Also note your successes and failures at school and work. *[Pause for writing after each paragraph]*

"On your timeline, put down names of friends you or the family had in school, work, the neighborhood, and the community. How did they affect your life? Do you stay in touch with any of them now? Who are your current friends? Are they family friends?

"Now note times when you remember laughing, especially in the family. Was there a favorite family joke? Remember your family's joyful and funny times.

"Include wonderful moments when you sensed you had a purpose or reason for living. Consider how this affected your life goals. These were steppingstones in your growth. Have you fulfilled them yet? What steps have you taken to achieve them? How do they influence your life today? What do you sense to be your purpose and goal in life now? If you do not have room on your timeline for all your answers, write them on other parts of your paper.

"Note strengths and abilities you exhibited in the past when confronted with problems. How did you solve these problems and what did you learn? Doing nothing is also a way to solve problems. Look at the choices you made, and see how each choice reflects a personal quality."

After everyone has done a personal timeline, get out a piece of shelf paper long enough for a family timeline. You may do this in the same session or in the next session. However, have everyone's timeline available whenever you make the family timeline.

Draw a line starting with the birth date of the oldest person present and extending ten to twenty years into the future. You may choose to put individual timelines on the chart or combine them into one.

You may also find it useful to add photographs to the chart or draw pictures of people and events on it. You will notice that the future is blank. To add a future to the timeline, make a collage of pictures family members cut from magazines or draw to represent the family's goals, qualities and hopes. Include all suggestions so that every person's possibilities are considered. After you have compiled and discussed the family timeline, you can put it in your family box or some place safe where you can take it out, review it, and add to it from time to time.

EXERCISE: FAMILY SYNTHESIS QUESTIONNAIRE

These questions look for family rituals, traditions, culture, successes, and character strengths, and emphasize the importance of remembering old stories and mottos of ancestors and building current family stories and songs. For example, children of parents who enjoyed reading and singing with them before bedtime may carry on the tradition by doing the same with their own children.

The questionnaire can be done in family gatherings or by members individually. Either way, writing down the answers is helpful for all family members, so have paper and pen or pencil available for each person. Allow time for those who have answered the questions individually to share their answers. Remember, each person's answers, including the children's, are acceptable and tell of their perception of the family and of their hopes and pains, their dreams and purpose. Since the questionnaire is long and detailed, it may be done over several meetings.

Start by writing down your family's last name or names and see if they have any special meaning or translation. Have these names been changed over the generations? Besides surnames, what are other names are common in your family of origin?

Now write down one word that describes your family today, and then start the questions. You may either write your answers individually before discussing them, or discuss them first, with one family member writing the answers down for all.

1. **HEROES:** Who are your family's heroes today? Whom do you admire most? Who were the people your grandparents and great-grandparents considered heroes? Go back through the generations

and find the stories of family heroes that have been passed down to you. How would a hero act in your family today? How does a hero handle adversity?

2. **BOOKS AND MYTHS:** What are your family's favorite books, poems, fairy tales, and myths? Is there a favorite story or myth that has been passed down through the generations? What is there about these family stories that makes them important? Are there stories that make you laugh, cry, or help you remember courage?

3. **THE ARTS:** Does your family have favorite pictures or statues? Do you have favorite buildings or monuments? Was there a favorite song or music that your mother, father, or grandparent used to sing or play? What was their favorite picture or music? Is there a building, picture, or a piece of music that would describe your family?

4. **SPORTS AND GAMES:** Does you family play sports or games, including card games, board games, and video games with each other? What about these sports or games do you like? What sports or games did your parents and grandparents play? Did any of these sports or games help your family cope with emergencies?

5. **MONEY:** How does you family handle money? If you had a lot of money, what would you do? If you had very little money, what would you do? How have your parents and grandparents used money? What have been the family's financial circumstances back though the generations? What techniques did your ancestors use to thrive or survive?

6. **FAMILY RULES:** What rules do you use in this family? What rules did your parents and grandparents use? Which rules are helpful in organizing your life with each other? Do your family rules change when others are present? Which rules would you like to pass on or not pass on to future generations?

7. **FRIENDSHIP:** What does friendship mean to your family? How does your family make friends? Do you keep friends a long time or a short time? What do you do to maintain relationships with your family and friends? What are the characteristics that you admire in your friends? Do you have these characteristics too?

8. **HARD TIMES:** What events have been difficult in your family? What events were difficult for your parents and grandparents? How did you cope and how did they cope with these events and what happened afterwards? What have you learned about yourself and your family from these hard times and your reactions to them? Have you learned ways to help you cope better? Do any unresolved feelings about the hard times still affect your family?

9. **GOOD TIMES:** What events have given your family happiness and joy? What have been happy events for your parents and grandparents? How did you react to or cope with those times and what happened afterwards? Do you remember the laughter and good feelings? See if you can imagine yourself and the family in a good time. What did you learn about yourself and your family from that time and your reaction to it? If you could describe happy events in the family with a single word or image, what would it be?

10. **TRADITIONS:** What are your family's holiday and birthday traditions? How did your parents and grandparents celebrate holidays and birthdays? What other traditions did your family celebrate? What is the oldest tradition that has been handed down in your family? If you could name a single celebration that best characterizes your family, what would it be? What tradition would you like your family to have?

11. **OCCUPATIONS:**

    Children: What kind of person would you like to be when you grow up? What kind of work would you like to do?

    Parents: When you were a child, what kind of person did you want to be and what kind of work did you want to do when you grew up?

    Parents and children: What is there about the occupations and the people you admired that was important to you? How would these occupations allow you to express yourself? What occupations were important to your parents, grandparents, and great-grandparents?

12. **STUDIES AND HOBBIES:** What studies, activities, or hobbies do you like? Do you like going to your school or job? What is there about your studies or hobbies that you like and don't like? What is there about these activities that allows you to express yourself? What are important activities and hobbies in your family and for your parents and grandparents? Is education important in your family?

13. **SPIRITUALITY:** What value does the spiritual have in your family? Does the family believe in a Higher Power, Spiritual Reality, Universal Mind, God, Allah, Yahweh, Buddha, or Jesus? Do you attend religious services? What were the beliefs of your parents, grandparents, and ancestors? If you were scared, or in a crisis, danger, or trouble, where would you go? Whom would you turn to? Do your beliefs help you?

14. **PURPOSE:** What is the purpose of having a family? What is the purpose of this family? What did your parents, grandparents, and ancestors see as their purpose in life? As you look over the generations, what was it that held them together or forced them apart? What did they want for themselves as their purpose in life, and what did they want for future generations? What purpose did each couple, family, and individual want to express to the world? How does knowing that there is Purpose in each individual and in the family help people cope with life's events?

15. **FUTURE:** What do you see happening in your family in the next month? In the next year? In five years? What would you like to have happen in your family? What would you like to see happen in your community or the world in this next year? How might your family express this wish? Develop a statement or motto your family would like to use this next year to express its wish for itself, the community,

and the world. Plan to say your statement every day for the rest of the year.

16. **QUALITIES:** What qualities have you received from your family? Examples are appreciation, brotherhood, calm, compassion, conviction, cooperation, courage, decisiveness, delight, discipline, faith, freedom, forgiveness, grace, gratitude, harmony, humor, joy, light, love, loyalty, patience, peace, persistence, power, simplicity, sisterhood, strength, truth, unity, wonder, vitality. What qualities does your family value? Which do they express and live? What qualities are you trying to develop? What were important qualities for past generations?

17. **STRENGTH AND WILL:** What is the dominant strength of this family? What do you do in crises to stay strong? What did your parents and grandparents do for strength? Was there a strong will in

your family in the past and how did the family express it? How does your family use its will? Does this family express good will? Does the family use its will skillfully? Can you tell of times that your family showed skillful will or loving will?

18. **SOUL:** What is your family's soul or unique gift that it has offered to the world over generations? How has this unique expression helped the world to be a better or different place? Is there a motto or statement that could express this gift from the past generations, through the present generations, and to future generations? Is this motto different or the same as the motto you chose in Question 15? See if you want to keep them separate or combine them. What would this motto mean to the world and how would it describe your family to the world? What is there about this motto that would allow each member to be resilient in the face of hardship?

19. **DREAMS:** What dreams does your family have? What were the dreams of past generations? It has been said that it is the ability to dream that makes humanity unique and important to the universe. What dreams have you had that you think might help the universe? What important dreams has your family had? What dreams of past generations changed the family? How have dreams helped you and the family identify your purpose?

20. **IDEAL MODEL:** What is your ideal model for a person? What is your ideal model for a family? What were your parents' and your grandparents' ideal models of a family? How does your ideal model express the soul, purpose, and motto of the family? After all family members have described their ideal model of the family, ask each person to stand in a central spot designated as the place of the ideal family model and describe what it feels like and what they want to do to make this model become more of a reality.

Once you have finished the questions, take a moment to have each family member jot down one word that describes your family now. Is this the same word that you wrote before you did the questions? If so, have your perceptions of the family changed at all?

Now write down one phrase or a memory of an event from your family that makes you smile.

These questions may take several family meetings and discussions. Allow time for family members to think about the questions and their answers again and again. It would be wonderful to review your answers in a year and see if they have changed. Writing down the answers, as suggested earlier, allows the family to reflect on them later.

Remember to put your questionnaire and your motto in your box along with the other important family items. You also might make a list of larger items such as a wedding veil, furniture, books, a particular piece of art and where they came from and to whom they should be willed. These items, kept in your home, will help your family connect with its history.

EXERCISE: THE FAMILY SHIELD

Having used the questionnaire, you may want to draw a family shield or coat of arms. In the questionnaire, you are asked about important family qualities and a family motto. These will be the basis for your shield. The motto will be on the shield, and qualities can be reflected in your choices of symbols in each section. If you need ideas, there are many books in libraries and bookstores on building family shields as the knights did in the Middle Ages.

Make your shield with three to five separate fields or sections, each in a color that has special meaning. One field might have animals, such as you discussed in the family meeting, another a picture of your house, another stars or other symbols to indicate how many people are in the family, and another section may have a family symbol for certain qualities that your family expresses. Consider also symbols from previous generations.

Whatever you put on your shield should indicate your uniqueness and have a positive meaning. Shields show not only how the family sees itself but also how the family wants the rest of the world to see it.

FAMILY DISIDENTIFICATION

Assagioli coined the term "disidentification" to describe a process that helps each of us become more aware of our personality elements and allows us to experience the truth of who we are. As he says:

"We are dominated by everything with which our self becomes identified. We can dominate and control everything from which we disidentify ourselves."

Many of our thoughts, feelings, and worries enslave us. When we allow ourselves to be dominated by depression and anger, Assagioli says, "We are put in chains." When our anxieties rule us, we become so unable to make choices that we freeze and stay stuck in our fear and pain. Only when we step back from, or objectify, our fears and addictions can we be free to see what is controlling us and what our choices are.

This stepping back is done not to deny our problems or dissociate from them. The object of disidentification is to see them more clearly along with all the choices we have and to re-identify with our deepest self.

We experience a similar process when we sleep and consciously let go of our concerns and unsolved problems and let our unconscious mind work. We often wake up with the answers. Thomas Alva Edison could not figure out how to keep the little wire inside the light bulb from burning up when the current ran through it. On waking one morning he realized that all he had to do was take the air out of the glass bulb. Today's incandescent light bulbs all feature a vacuum for the wire.

To help us experience and use disidentification, Assagioli developed an exercise to show us how overly identified we can be with our bodies, physical appearances, and diseases; our emotions, including those we deny, and our thoughts, which can be obsessive, uncreative, and running wild. The exercise helps us see and experience the beginnings of many of our problems. Often our perceptions and habits have physical, emotional, and mental components. The greater the emotional and physical experience, the greater the likelihood we will repeat old defense mechanisms in times of threat. Disidentification helps us step behind our defenses and experiences to see what choices we want to make about any life situation. It takes us back into our most fundamental reality, our consciousness.

EXERCISE: INDIVIDUAL DISIDENTIFICATION

Find a quiet chair where there are no distractions, and get a journal or tablet to write on later. Sit comfortably with your feet on the ground and back straight but not rigid. Get in touch with your choice to be here at this time. Breathe comfortably and be aware of your body. Let go of any tensions. Feel alert and relaxed.

Mentally scan your body and say to yourself, "I have a body. I live in this body in sickness and health. It is a precious instrument of experience in the world. I am grateful for this body, grateful to be alive. But I am more than my body." *[Pause]*

Review your different emotions over the last day or so. Allow yourself to fully experience them. Don't hold back. Say, "I have emotions. There are no bad emotions. They often protect me and help me more fully experience the world. I can step back from them and not be overwhelmed by them, for I am more than my emotions, just as I am more than my body." *[Pause]*

After you have disidentified from your emotions and your body, observe your thoughts. Say, "I have thoughts. Sometimes they seem undisciplined, just so much chatter, and controlled by anxieties. Sometimes I can focus them. I can do that now. I can find a quiet corner in my mind and realize that I am more than my body, more than my emotions, and more than my thoughts. I am a center of awareness, consciousness, and self-realization. *[Pause]*

"From this center, I can look at my body and see what it needs. *[Pause]* Now I can choose to direct it in achieving its greatest health. From this center I can see what my emotions need. *[Pause]* Now I can allow my emotions to be peaceful and express them with purpose.

"From this center, I can marvel at my mind and see the qualities of who I really am. I see purpose and potential in my life. I can experience a light, a radiance filling my mind and my heart."

Taking a deep breath and, enjoying the quiet, write about what you have experienced. In a day or two reread what you wrote about your experience and add anything more you want.

Practicing this exercise individually will help all family members become more aware of their bodies, emotions, and thoughts. They will start to realize that they have a day-to-day waking consciousness, a center of consciousness, the self or "I", which is in touch with all their unconscious processes and potentials. This exercise not only unleashes creative understandings for daily living; it also strengthens purpose and builds resilience for times of crisis.

BETTY'S STORY

Betty had a problem with her relationship with her father. She had experienced him as emotionally abusive and highly critical of her. She was unable to talk to him and felt inadequate and "stupid" in his presence. When he was in the hospital receiving treatment for cancer, she wanted to achieve some resolution to their relationship. She decided to go to see him at the hospital and take her sister with her. While there, all she could do was sing him songs. She still perceived him as cold and forbidding, and her fear kept her from talking to him.

She so deeply wanted to talk to him that she came into therapy. In her first month of therapy she began to talk to him but still couldn't fully maintain her self-identity when she was with him. She described her fear as consuming her thoughts and determining her actions.

In a therapy session after he died, Betty did the disidentification exercise, stepping back from her fear, observing it, and seeing what it looked like. She described her fear as a big snarling dog. She remembered that when she was a child, a big dog chased her and she ran home frightened. As she grew older and learned to bike, stay quiet, and stand her ground, she noticed that dogs would leave her alone and move away. As she was describing her fear, she realized that she had seen her father as a frightening dog, and she thought that if she were quiet, he too would leave her alone and would not be so frightening. Her behavior had created a distance between them.

Betty also realized that she was afraid not only of her father's power but also of her own power. Fearful of being like her father and hurting others, she backed off any time she might have asserted herself. Yet she also knew that he was very well-liked and had many friends. By disidentifying from her fear, she realized that she thought she had only two choices in life—be timid or be feared. She saw that her father could synthesize the two opposites and act himself with others and be loved. By observing this process and re-identifying with her self, Betty understood that she too could experience a similar synthesis and choose to live more fully in relationship with others.

As the disidentification exercise helps each individual, a family version of it helps the family. The same principles are followed as the family learns to disidentify from problems inside and outside of it. In the following exercise each family member experiences his or her identity in the family and the family's identity in the world.

EXERCISE: FAMILY DISIDENTIFICATION

This exercise can be done with several generations or only the nuclear family. Everyone will need to have paper and pen or pencil handy. If some family members cannot get out of a chair or stand for a length of time, tell them to use their imaginations to follow the standing part of the exercise.

Seat the family in a circle with enough space in the center that the family can stand together in it.

LEADER:

"Slowly quiet your body, your emotions, and your mind. Center yourself and get in touch with your choice to be here in this room at this time. As each of us quiets, see that in the center of our circle is the center of our family, which is its deepest identity and purpose. *[Pause]*

"Come back to your body and say to yourself, 'I live in my body in this family. My body may look like one of my parent's, some other family member's, or no one in the family. Whatever my body characteristics, my body is good and important to this family. My body is a precious instrument of expression, growth, and potential in this family and in the world. Each of the bodies in this family is important and has a unique expression and purpose for this family. How does my body express this family? What does it need from other members of the family? We all have bodies, but we are even more than our family body.' Stop and write what you have learned. *[Pause for writing]*

"Now see what your emotions or feelings are when in the family. Say to your emotions, 'I have emotions in this family. Some of my feelings are in reaction to others, and some are my own family feelings. Some feelings may not be allowed in my family, but I know that I can experience love, anger, sorrow, fear, joy, frustration, embarrassment, and many more emotions. Having all these emotions makes us more sensitive and human to each other and others. We all have emotions, but we are even more than the family body and the family emotions.' *[Pause]*

"Now see what thoughts you have when you are in the family. Say to your mind, 'I have a mind with many family thoughts. I observe how others think, and I see how we get common thoughts. I see how our thoughts can stop each other or can build the family and its expression into the future. I realize that each of us is part of the mind of the family, and yet each of us has our own body, emotions, and thoughts, yet we are more." Take a few minutes to write about your emotions and thoughts. *[Pause for writing]*

"Now let's all of us get up from our chairs and stand in a place that we will call the family center or 'I'.

"Breathe deeply in this center. Feel its love and acceptance of the family. Quiet yourself more and imagine that you can look back on your body sitting in your chair, and say to yourself:

"'I disidentify from my body in my chair and re-identify with the family center. From this family center, I can see that the family also has a body made up of different sexes, ages, heights, weights, and other physical characteristics. Together we look a certain way that even follows us when we are apart.'

"How can this family work together to get its needs met and its potential realized? How does this family express itself physically into the world?' Return to your seat and write your insights. *[Pause for writing]*

"Staying seated and using your imagination to see yourself still in the family center, look back at your own family emotions and see what they are. What are the family choices for expressing emotions? How does the family see the world emotionally? Write down what you have learned. *[Pause]*

"Now look back on your family thoughts, and get in touch with the family mind. How does this family think? What does this family think others think about it? What does the family mind need from each of its members and from the family center? Write all of this down." *[Pause]*

After everyone has finished, ask them to share their insights about the family and their own needs in the family. After the sharing, ask all of the family members to stand again together in the family center.

LEADER, *continuing:*

"Allow yourself to experience this family center as if you are standing in a beam of light coming down on each of you standing here. As you stand in this light and love, see what the family needs.

> "See the uniqueness of the family over generations and the need of the world for this family to express its "I", its special identity and purpose. See this understanding shining in each family member. Thank the family Self and the light, and experience the love between each of you."

THE JONES FAMILY

The Jones family came into therapy because Linda, the youngest of the three children, was having a difficult time in school and was withdrawn and argumentative with her siblings. She felt her older siblings were more successful, and she saw herself as a failure. In turn, her parents felt like failures, blaming themselves for Linda's unhappiness. The family was taught the disidentification exercise.

After everyone used the disidentification exercise, Linda felt free enough to tell her family about her problems with school work, especially reading. She was embarrassed when asked to read out loud and often could not comprehend what she read. She was embarrassed because her siblings could read easily and she could not. It became evident to the family that Linda had dyslexia, a reading problem, and that she had tried to hide it rather than share it with her family. The exercise gave her a chance to disidentify from her pain and admit to her family what was causing her trouble.

At the end of the exercise, the family praised Linda for her intelligence and her courage to reveal the cause of her pain. Her revelation allowed her parents to get her tutoring and to realize that they were not to blame for her problems. The whole family became Linda's allies with her at school and at home. Linda went on to graduate from college and become a successful teacher who can quickly understand any child who struggles with learning disabilities.

The disidentification exercise can also be helpful with couples.

MARGE AND JIM'S STORY

When Marge and Jim came into marital counseling, he complained that she always criticized him, and she complained that he didn't love her and didn't listen to her. After they did the disidentification exercise, stood up, and stepped away from their seats, the pain between them became very clear to them. Asked to leave the pain back in their seats and see what they wanted from the marriage, they found it hard not to keep re-identifying with their pain. When they finally disidentified from it, Marge saw how she had her mother's sharp tongue, and Jim saw how he had become like his withdrawn father. As they started to identify with their marital self, their marital center, they could see some of the love and potentials for both of them in the marriage. They saw that instead of living out their parents' mistakes, they could have their own marriage and identities. They also decided to have a family meeting with their children and talk about not only past family marriages but also what they and the children could build together.

MEDITATION

The disidentification exercise can also be useful as an introduction to individual and family meditation. Assagioli recommends meditation as a way of deepening the experiences and insights of his exercises and integrating the personality. Many people use prayer, particularly repetitive prayer, as their form of meditation. They find it calms them and allows them to center and let go of their everyday life. Certainly, having a regular prayer life or meditation time gives one a discipline to aid resilience when life offers its hardships.

It would be helpful for the family to set aside a quiet place at home where members can sit alone or together when they need to calm themselves or sit in silence, focusing on breathing to settle the mind and let go of emotional distractions.

This is the beginning of mindfulness, which Assagioli recommends as a necessary prelude to meditation. He describes mindfulness as a skill similar to disidentification but with emphasis on awareness and control of the mind while observing events, emotions, thoughts, and physical experiences in the present moment without trying to stop or prolong any of them, just nonjudgmentally observing and experiencing them at the same time. If a bothersome thought or physical experience occurs, the person disidentifies from it and re-identifies with their center and their breathing.

Mindfulness helps people become aware of their habitual destructive behaviors, emotional outbursts, and obsessive thoughts and start making choices about how they behave. Like disidentification, mindfulness is a practiced awareness that can be with us at all times and that can be called upon in any stressful situation.

Once people have learned mindfulness, Assagioli says, they are ready to move on to the three kinds of meditation—reflective, receptive, and creative.

In reflective meditation, we treat our mind as an instrument that we can train to serve us when we need clarity. We start by focusing our mind and observing our thinking process. We keep going even when we think we have fully explored a subject. This way we discover new aspects of any subject we wish to explore.

Through this active observation and evaluation, we find out more and more about ourselves and see creative and positive alternatives. If emotions, bodily sensations, or intrusive thoughts start to take over this process, we disidentify from them and ask them why they are present and what they are trying to tell us. Objectifying and disidentifying allows us to hear what these parts of us are trying to tell us. They may hold a key in our process. After we get the insight from any of these, we thank them and then refocus our meditation on the subject at hand.

In receptive meditation, we listen, allowing ourselves to be spoken to, rather than just trying to observe and see. The object is to be so quiet that we can receive an intuition, inspiration, message, or stimulus for action without our personality interrupting it. So we start with an inner silence and stillness. To still the mind, it helps to use a word or phrase that elicits an image of calm and peace. If you use prayer for meditation, you might repeat a simple blessing or phrase such as:

- "Let the Self guide and direct my life."
- "Let God show me the way."
- "Let Light guide my path."
- "God is Love and Light."
- "The Lord is my Shepherd, I shall not want."
- "Al Rahmon or Al Raheem," a Muslim payer to a compassionate and merciful Allah.
- Or you can concentrate on a quality (see Appendix I), or imagine a quiet place that feels blessed.

Sometimes we "see" the messages in our mind's eye. Sometimes we "hear" or sense them in our body. Usually these understandings come with simplicity or sureness, sometimes bringing an inner smile. Assagioli describes these as experiences of "contact," almost of being touched, as affirming and recharging senses of Presence and inner nearness.

Assagioli warns that sometimes we are aware fairly quickly of having received an understanding, vivid and clear but quickly vanishing, so immediately writing down the intuition helps. Other times we experience a "delayed reception," after we sit many times in our meditation or prayer waiting and seeming to receive nothing. Then, when we are doing a totally different activity, the understanding will suddenly come to us. Therefore at the close of your prayer or meditation, maintain an inner attitude of watchful waiting, openness, and faith that your meditation is being heard.

In creative meditation we modify and transform our personality by looking at our motives, making choices for our good, and clarifying our ideas to form a new personality around our center.

Assagioli says the time spent meditating should be short at first and that the theme should vary. He suggests rotating themes weekly or monthly. He adds that group meditation helps concentration and integration and that the group sharing can create a sense of group identity. The same can be said for family meditation and the building of resilience. Certainly the Quakers have found this to be true as they sit in Silence together waiting for Truth to become known.

After any kind of meditation, to ground the understanding gained, it helps to make an affirmation. Examples:

- "God is now active in our life."
- "We are patient and kind."
- "We can move forward in our lives."
- "We can see the love in each person we meet."
- "We can express our family identity in the world."

The affirmation should come directly out of the understanding received. After the family has done an exercise or meditation and received an understanding, it is important to write down the affirmation, say it, and post it for all to remember. Be aware, though, that affirmations may change as the family grows, understands, and integrates with its "I". Meditation, affirmations, and prayer should not get static but should always be open to new understanding and growth.

The only consistent and unchanging affirmation is thanksgiving. After each meditation or exercise, whether personal or family, even if there is a delayed answer to the reflection, each person needs to give thanks for the Self, God, Presence, or Universal that is always with us and present when we ask and are ready to receive. Families should also thank each member for participating and bringing his or her Self and presence to each meeting.

FAMILY SELF

When we, as individuals and families, understand who we really are and can accept our inherited traits and values, we can experience resilience and get in touch with our authentic identity. To describe who we are, Assagioli developed an egg diagram that maps the human psyche. The diagram assumes the integrity of human physical and psychological systems and an interaction of conscious experience and unconscious forces. It is important to remember that this is a map, a guide, a mere approximation of the psyche's riches.

THE EGG DIAGRAM

In this diagram, Assagioli sees the human psyche as made up of seven parts:

1. The **Lower Unconscious** is the seat of phobias, compulsions, primitive urges, fundamental drives, intense emotional complexes, paranoid delusions, and negative dreams. It is the place of past memories and injuries, alive with wounds, aggressions, and physical urges. Assagioli calls the energy of the lower unconscious a "life force" that, when denied or traumatized, develops defenses.

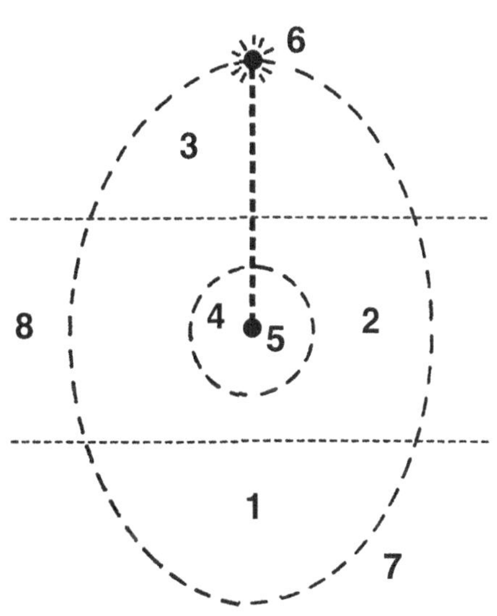

2. The **Middle Unconscious** holds our more easily accessible and recent experiences,

memories, and thoughts. It is in this region that imagination elaborates thoughts and develops ideas that are close to the surface of consciousness. This area works through our personality to help us understand what is occurring in the present.

3. In the center of the middle unconscious is the **Field of Consciousness** and the **"I"**, or conscious self. The field of consciousness is that place of immediate awareness, or as Assagioli says, of "the incessant flow of sensations, images, thoughts, feelings, desires and impulses which we can observe, analyze, and judge."

4. The conscious self, or **"I"**, is an integrating center of pure awareness and consciousness, without content. It is the personal self that we know as us, the locus of our individuality in our body that can access all elements of our personality, mind, feelings, and body, yet it is distinct from the personality. It is active, unifying, empathic, introspective, and dynamic. The "I" is the lamp through which the light, Purpose, and potentials of the Higher Self can penetrate our personality. Through awareness of and interaction and familiarity with this center, we gain our resilience.

5. The **Higher Unconscious** is, according to Assagioli, the region of our "higher intuitions, inspirations, ethical imperatives, humanitarian and heroic actions, altruistic love, genius, illumination, and ecstasy." It is the area of our highest psychic functions, where our potentials and truest qualities already exist, ready to emerge in our lives.

6. The **Higher Self** is the very soul of us, all we are and more. It is the luminous source, the soul plan, the truest creation that has chosen to incarnate into this life, and yet it is always in touch with all creation, the Universal, or the Creator. It projects itself into the personality through the self, or "I" but can speak to any other part of us it wishes to influence. Like its Creator, it is always invested in the revelation and wonder of who we are and were created to be. Assagioli calls it the "organizing principle of life."

7. The **Collective Unconscious** is all of the ancestral and cultural archetypes that are both outside and inside us in all levels of the unconscious, as well as in the culture and family around us.

Note that in the diagram, all the lines are dotted to show the influence of each area on the others within our own body and personality and outside of us and the interchange among them. We are bio-psycho-spiritual-ecological systems with internal and external interactions.

The egg diagram describes every individual from birth through life. At any one time, all aspects of our unconscious are influencing our actions as well as our perceptions. So, while we are working with a relationship, pondering a problem, doing our jobs, or socializing with our friends, our actions and desires are influenced by our past experiences, the present, and our potentials for the future. Assagioli says that we often struggle harder against who we are and can be than against all the negative of who we have been. The negative is more familiar and less frightening than what we perceive as risk in being our real intrinsic self. Ironically the true Self is stronger and has more energy than all the defenses.

THE FAMILY EGG DIAGRAM

Family Synthesis assumes that families have the same systemic integrity and the same conscious and unconscious rules as individuals. A family is a whole unit with the different members acting to maintain it and with dynamic patterns of relationships, some inherited over generations, all bearing the potential for growth and healing. Therefore, we can map the family egg diagram like the individual's.

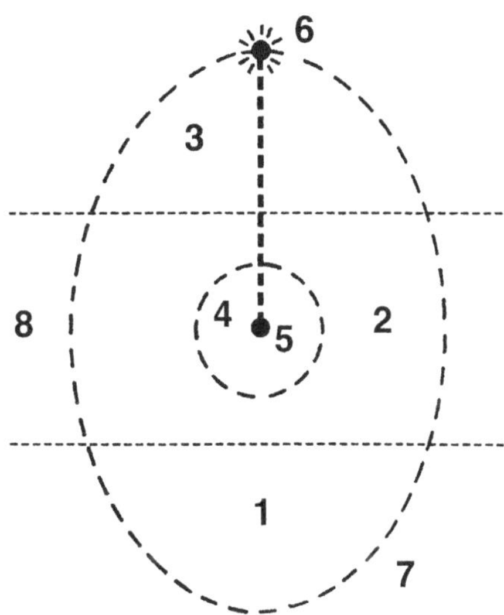

1. The **Family Lower Unconscious** houses physical needs and desires. Survival, procreation, and the strong energy to exist are here, but so is the energy to exist as a family always has. Here are the complexes, traumas, prejudices, and abuses handed down through the generations. You've heard it said:
   - "Do it this way because this is how the Kellys have always treated family and outsiders."

- "My father beat the tar out of me, so I am going to do that to my children. Make 'em strong."
- "I'll show my daughters how women should treat men so that they will know how to be a wife."

These beliefs, fears, and ways of behaving become rigid over the generations. They become world views, social boundaries, and complexes that can limit growth, and each new marriage and child brings forth all the old family expectations, projections, and strivings.

2. The **Family Middle Unconscious** is where the family members live from one day to the next and act out their roles. Each member has not only a birth and generational role but also a specific role in relation to others in the family system. Experts say that when a dysfunctional child is taken out of a family, another child, even the family hero, becomes dysfunctional in the same way, keeping the family exactly the same. Each person becomes a way for the family unconscious to express itself. Each, living the past in the present and hoping for the future, acts out the family personality.
3. The **Family Field of Consciousness** is the area of readily accessible memories and everyday interactions and communications between the family members and others.
4. The family **"I"**, or family self, is the conscious reflection of the family Higher Self. It is the family's active, integrating center, regulating the various parts of the family personality, bringing the family closer to its Purpose in society and creation. While each member expresses just a part of the whole, each is important to the family purpose, and all members play their parts throughout life.
5. The **Family Higher Unconscious** is the area of becoming, where family qualities are emerging or waiting to emerge. It is the area of potentials, inspirations, humanitarian urges, heroic actions, and higher intuitions. The potentials are the family's evolutionary future, helping it express its unique identity, meaning, and Purpose for the world. As the family discovers these, it finds the energy to express them together and individually.

6. The **Family Higher Self** guides the family "I", or self, in realizing the family's highest potentials and taking its unique place in advancing society. By recognizing its Self, the family can integrate around its core of meaning and Purpose and come into coherence with the Universal and the essential relatedness of all things. The family Self is the synthesis of all this family's relationships in life that have been, are, and are becoming.
7. The **Family Collective Unconscious** consists of the family's ancestral structures and archetypes as well as society's cultural, social, and national myths, beliefs, and motifs. These are instinctive, with the power to influence our perceptions of ourselves and the world and to affect all of our family relationships—how people treat each other in marriage, how parents and children act toward one another, who we consider family, and how a family interacts with other families. Some families harden their boundaries like armor and try not to allow information in but, in doing so, stunt their growth. Being aware of the environment and willing to accept information from it gives a family a chance both to change and to influence the environment.

EXERCISE: WALKING THE FAMILY EGG DIAGRAM

For this exercise, the family needs space so that members can get up and move through the different unconscious levels and experience the different roles they play. The family will also need places to sit and write.

Before you start the exercise, choose parts of the room for the different parts of the egg diagram and note, especially, the place of the "I". The exercise is active, with standing and walking to different parts of the room. Some family members may get tired and need more time to sit, but they can use their imaginations to do the exercise. Each person needs to have pen and paper ready for journaling or making notes.

LEADER:

"As a family, stand in the middle of the room, in the space you have chosen for the family "I". Take a few minutes to quiet, relax, and fully experience what it is like to be in this family center. See if you can get a sense of family purpose and identity. Stand in the quiet and listen to what is here in the center. *[Pause to allow everyone time to center.]*

"As a group, move to a space that you have designated for the family lower unconscious. Here is the life force of the family and memories of past mistakes, successes, and roles you have played in the family at different ages. Note to yourself these roles and what it feels like in your body as you remember what happened and how you reacted. What emotions do you have in this place? What thoughts and images come to your mind? Go back to your seat and briefly write your observations. *[Pause]*

"Stand again in the center or family "I". Let go of the experience of the past and yet remember the survival instinct in you and your family as you see the past traumas. From this family center, see how the lower unconscious influences other parts of the family. Get a sense of what past roles are still alive in the family today. Get quiet and calm in this center. Identify again with the family purpose in this center and see what family qualities you are now beginning to be aware of. *[Pause for reflection or writing.]*

"You are starting to see the family roles each person plays away from the center. So now move to the area designated for the middle unconscious. In the middle unconscious are our subpersonalities, or the roles we play in this family.

"Since each person has specific roles, move to what you consider to be one of your family roles, or family subpersonalities. You may be a son, daughter, brother, sister, parent, spouse, step-parent, relative, worker, student, or one of many other roles. Remember your role may be far out from the center; it may be closer to the lower unconscious, the middle unconscious, or even the Higher Unconscious. Move to where you think this role now occurs in the family. If necessary, move around the room until you feel you are in the right place for your family role. See if you are near anyone else, or if you are far from everyone else in the family. *[Pause for everyone to see where everyone else is.]*

"Standing in this role, fully experience how it feels in your body. Are you tense or stiff or are you relaxed? Do you feel healthy or sick? Do you have a sense in your body of how old you were when you started in this role?

"What are your feelings in this role? Are you happy? Sad? Angry? Frustrated? Scared? Can you feel independently, or do your feelings depend on what other family members are feeling? Do your feelings influence how others feel and think about you and themselves?

"Look at your thoughts when you are in this role. Are they your own or determined by how other family members think? What is your view of others outside your family? Do people outside your family change your thoughts about yourself, your role, or your family? Fully experience what it is like to be in this family role. Can you get a sense of the purpose of this role? What quality does this role want to express? *[Pause]*

"Now think of another role you play in your family, and walk around the room into that role. Again see how your body experiences this role. Are you stiff? Relaxed? Healthy? Sick? How old are you?

"Fully experience your emotions in this second role. Are you happy? Angry? Sad? Frustrated? Scared? Withdrawn? How much do your feelings depend on others in the family?

"Now look at your thoughts in this second role. How do you think about yourself and others in the family? Do you continuously think about how other family members judge you and have expectations for you? How does the family influence your world view and your beliefs? Do you get a sense of the purpose of this role for yourself and your family?

"Go back to the center. Breathe deeply. Close your eyes and let go of the roles and feelings you have just had. Just become more of the center of this family. What is it like here in the center after you let go of the lower unconscious and your roles, or subpersonalities? In turn, each of you say out loud one or two words to describe how it is here. From this center, is there any communication between the center and the roles you play? What would need to happen for the different roles to listen to the center? Breathe in this awareness. *[Pause to write of the experience so far.]*

"Now all stand and move forward into the family Higher Unconscious. Everyone experience the qualities and potentials for this family. Say some of these qualities out loud. Say what quality you represent in this family. Some of the qualities you will recognize as already in the family and some are just coming into your awareness. Allow yourselves to more fully see what this family is, can be, and is becoming.

"Go back to the center, the family "I". Allow yourself to be even more aware of the family center, the family's different aspects, and the richness of its past, present, and future. As you stand here in the center, allow yourself to experience a light above your heads, a star or a sun, shining down on this center. Experience the love and peace that is in this ray of light. Experience the Purpose for this family that is in this ray of light. The Purpose may come as a body sensation, a feeling, an image, a thought, or a word. Breathe deeply of this experience.

"As you sit or stand in the family Purpose and beam of light, see this light go up and over your home. See it shining down on your family and where you live. Go still higher and see it shining down on your neighborhood and your state. See the light over the country. From higher still, imagine looking down on the world and seeing all the lights from all the homes, neighborhoods, and countries sparkling and shining out into space.

"As you look down on the Earth and all the families of the world, say to yourselves as slowly as possible, 'peace, peace, peace' and then 'love, love, love'. Follow with an 'amen' or 'so be it.' See yourself coming back down into your country and neighborhood, your home, the room you are in, and your body. Breathe deeply and allow time to truly bring all you have experienced into your body, feelings, and mind. Gently open your eyes if they are closed, look at the other family members, and see the light shining above each head and in everyone's eyes. Breathe deeply and just experience this moment.

"Go to your seat and your journal. Write or draw about this experience. Write about being in the lower unconscious, about what your roles in this family are, and about the Higher Unconscious and the family potential. Write about being in the center and what the family's Purpose is."

After everyone is done, let each person share whatever they wish.

EXERCISE: WHO AM "I" AS A FAMILY

The purpose of this exercise is for the family to further explore the family "I". This again emphasizes that the family is a unit, or system, with its own identity, purpose, and "I".

Have everyone seated with paper or journal and pen in hand.

LEADER:

"On your paper write the numbers one to twenty-five down the left hand side. Beside each number, write a brief phrase or word to describe your family. *[Pause for all to complete this task.]*

"Now put a star or check mark by the five most important descriptions. *[Pause for all to write.]*

"Now put an X by the single most important word or phrase for the family."

The leader collects all the papers.

"I have all your words and phrases about the family. If I were to throw away all these papers, what would the family be? Who is the family? What is left?" *[Pause for discussion]*

"As each of you sits in your seat, get in touch with the family "I" that is all your descriptions and more. Quietly see that the family "I", reflecting the Self, radiates its identity, purpose, and qualities, especially love, into the family. Just be quietly aware of the Self's existence."

QUALITIES

In the Higher Unconscious are aspects of the Self—inspirations, spiritual urges, and connections to a source of higher feelings and psychic functions, spiritual energies, potential growth patterns, latent talents, Purpose and values. We use the term "qualities" to describe these energies toward service and love. The Higher Unconscious also contains patterns for synthesis and integration of the personality and self with the Self. When we say someone has a good quality of life, we may mean certain material goods and ease, but true quality of life is a deep experience of connection with and expression of Self, of who we really are.

Psychosynthesis emphasizes the constant development or integration of all levels of the person or group with the "I" and the Self. It is a process or journey through life, an actualization of the Self through the person or group. For this reason we often see the qualities of the Higher Unconscious as aspects that we both have and yet are striving to express more and more into our life.

In the Family Synthesis Questionnaire, you answered a question about your family qualities. There is a similar list, with more qualities in Appendix I. Review them, adding other qualities that you have since seen or are beginning to see in your family and in each other.

EXERCISE: FAMILY QUALITIES

This exercise is designed to explore one quality and make the family more aware of its existence in the family. Participants will need paper to record their answers.

LEADER:

"Take a few minutes to quiet and center. In the silence allow yourself to think of a quality, any quality, taking the first one that occurs to you. Write the name of the quality on the top of your paper. Take time to focus on and experience this quality.

"Now start writing definitions of this quality. How would you describe it? When and where do you find it? What does it mean? How do you know when you have it? Just keep writing descriptions of your quality. If your mind wanders, take a deep breath and come back to focusing on your quality and write more.

"Take your time writing and begin to open up to the experience of this quality. What is the essence of this quality? Is there another quality that is deep inside your quality? Experience your quality fully by saying to yourself, 'I am______________ (quality).' Say it several times slowly, fully experiencing this quality.

"Slowly allow yourself to become aware of sitting in the family circle. Someone start and say their 'I am_____________' statement. After each person does this, be quiet a few moments and, as a family, experience that quality in that person and in the family. Then go on to the next person."

It is important to allow family members time to fully explore and experience whatever quality they have chosen before the family shares together. For young children, one session will probably be enough; adults may enjoy more time.

As you share, sense what happens in the room as you focus on qualities, and see what quality begins to emerge that is part of all the other qualities.

EXERCISE: THE MOUNTAIN

Allow the family time to quiet and center, sitting in comfortable chairs and readying themselves for a journey in their imagination. They will not need to write until the end. The leader will need to go slowly, allowing family members to fully paint the terrain in their minds.

LEADER:

"See yourself and your family in a beautiful field. It is a perfect day with the sun warm overhead and the air a perfect temperature. A light breeze gently moves the grasses and wildflowers. Take time to fully enjoy this lovely open place and the warmth of the day.

"As you are looking around the field and taking in its beauty, see that there is a path winding through it and pointing toward the hill and, behind it, a mountain. Take in both the gentle rise of the hill and the sharper rise of the mountain. Imagine that, as a family, you come together and start walking on the path through the field rising to the hill.

"As you walk up the hill, realize that being together makes the rise seem easy. As you top the hill, realize that it is the first step to climbing the mountain ahead. Stay together and now start up the steeper path of the mountain. The path jogs and has cut-backs. Little streams cross it. Sometimes it is moss and dirt, other times gravel. *[Pause]*

"The family hike has become difficult, with some having a harder time than others keeping up. Help each other with whatever talent and strength you have and they need.

"Ahead of you on the steep path, a large boulder blocks your way. How will your family handle this obstacle? What do you do when your way is blocked? Using your imagination and intuition, see your family succeeding in finding a way around the boulder. When you get to the other side, see how you experience each other. Thank each other.

"Continue on the steep path, going through a forest but seeing ahead the top of the mountain beyond the trees. As you ascend, realize that among the rocks, there is life—mosses, grasses, and flowers in some of the crevices. Your path is high now, steeper, and leads to the top. As a group, finish climbing to the top, bringing along the stragglers, the breathless, and those with hurt feet. Standing at the top, feel the cool air. Experience the brightness and warmth of the sun pouring down on all of you and filling your very beings. Feel its power, love, and Purpose for your family. Enjoy being here on the top of the mountain. *[Pause]*

"From the top of this mountain, look out on the vast expanse of the world. See other mountain tops, family groups on them, and the sun shining on all these different people.

"Breathe deeply again of the mountain air, and, filled with light and Purpose. Now turn to walk back down the mountain. As you start down, realize how effortless the path has become compared with the steep upward journey. As you progress lower down the path, see that in front of you, in the field, what you thought were flowers are the faces of many people. The people are welcoming you, your family, and the Purpose you have brought with you back into the world. You recognize some of the faces as friends, neighbors, and relatives and others as people you hardly know or have yet to meet. All are overjoyed to see you come home and take what you have learned into the world.

"Before you stop to write of your journey and all you have learned today, say thank you to the family Self that has been here as your guide to who you all really are."

FAMILY SUBPERSONALITIES

Like our individual "I", the family "I" uses many roles, or subpersonalities, in interacting with others inside and outside the family. Subpersonalities are habits, traits, perceptions, and experiences that get combined into behavioral patterns that help us adjust to crises, new information, or perceived family or personal needs. Any time we experience sickness, injury, or emotional distress, it automatically excites in us the same intense physical, emotional, and intellectual defense mechanisms we used in the past in similar situations.

At the center of each subpersonality is an original good intent and a quality seeking expression, so no subpersonality is inherently bad. But bad behavior is learned, often in our family, making it very hard to get back to that original intent or quality.

If we added some subpersonalities to the egg diagram, it might look like this:

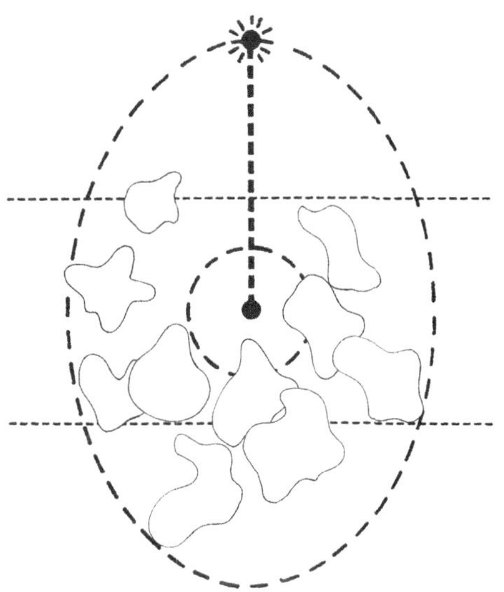

Notice that some of the subpersonalities come from the lower unconscious, some are located in the middle unconscious and are very accessible and present-oriented, and some have aspects of the potentials of the Higher Unconscious. Also see that some of the subpersonalities are close to the "I" and can accept direction from it, while others are much farther away, out of touch with our central identity, and possibly antagonistic to it. Some of our subpersonalities are large and dominant, while others are weak and seldom used.

Some subpersonalities have behaviors that are good and successful adaptations, the servants of who we really are, and some are dysfunctional and rigid, getting in our way as we try to adapt to changes in our circumstances. Often we keep a subpersonality and its behavior because we believe this is how our family wants us to behave.

Our subpersonalities may conflict with each other or work together. Some are determined by other groups or society, and some reflect who we are essentially, our "I". The latter allow us the greatest chance to be resilient in the face of trauma and change.

The National Council on Alcoholism and Drug Abuse describes some of these more rigid family patterns seen in the children of addicted parents. When the parents deny their problem, their children often adjust by hiding who they really are and develop subpersonalities that are rigid, fearful, and defensive. One role for these children is the hero, the child who wishes to be perfect, is a high achiever, but never feels good enough. Another is the scapegoat, the family troublemaker, hurt, guilty, disruptive, and argumentative. The mascot is the family clown, with exaggerated emotional responses, who tries to avoid family angers or confrontations. The lost child has no opinions or emotions, avoids close relationships, is easily overlooked, and is uncomfortable with any kind of attention.

Some of our greatest pain, depression, and anxiety occur when parts of us resist the "I" and the urgings from the Self. Families and individuals often repress the urge to be better and greater, to be creative, to serve, and to allow and accept differences. We are frightened that if we show our authentic self, our "I", or allow ourselves to grow and change, we will open ourselves to criticism and disappoint others. As a result, we repress the sublime and our uniqueness as much as our basic physical instincts. Resilience demands adapting to change, being centered, and knowing who we are. In order to understand who we are, we need to know all aspects of ourselves, including the parts we don't like.

Assagioli coined the term "subpersonality" based on what William James called our "various selves," or "functions," that are separate from our whole person. Others have described these as subconscious personalities, or ego states, separate from each other, detached from the core self, arising in response to the environment or some inner need, bound together by some common principle, and expressing themselves in specific behaviors.

Without using the term, writers for thousands of years have described subpersonalities. Greek mythology is full of stories of gods representing different aspects of ourselves and warring with each other for domination and power, just as our subpersonalities struggle with each other over who will be the boss.

Similarly, the psalms of the Hebrew Bible express not only Israel's struggles but also the writer's inner ones. When he cries out against the pursuers, foes, and enemies who taunt and scheme against him, he is talking about his own subpersonalities and his desires that tempt him away from his spiritual nature, or "I". Listen to him:

- "O Lord my God, in you I take refuge; save me from all my pursuers, and deliver me, or like a lion they will tear me apart; they will drag me away, with no one to rescue." (Psalm 7, verses 1-2)
- "O Lord, how many are my foes! Many are rising against me; many are saying to me, 'There is no help for you in God.' But you, O Lord, are a shield around me, my glory, and the one who lifts up my head. I cry aloud to the Lord, and he answers me from his holy hill." (Psalm 3, verses 1-4)
- "Teach me your way, O Lord, and lead me on a level path because of my enemies. Do not give me up to the will of my adversaries, for false witnesses have risen against me, and they are breathing out violence." (Psalm 27, Verses 11-12)

On and on, the psalmist writes about the strength of the Lord and His Mercy to overcome and answer those who call on Him. When the psalmist vanquishes his enemies and aligns himself with his Self, his spiritual nature, he writes songs of praise and gratitude.

Fairy tales also illustrate the struggle between the self and subpersonalities. Cinderella is a good example. Her subpersonalities are her ugly step-sisters, cruel stepmother, loving father, blessed dead mother, and wise fairy godmother. Her family home, where she is a drudge, and the palace, where she is a beautiful princess, also represent facets of her.

A more modern example is *The Wizard of Oz*, with all the parts of Dorothy represented by good and bad witches, munchkins, a cowardly lion, a brainless scarecrow, a tin man without a heart, and a very human but wise wizard. As Dorothy finds her courage and will to survive, her subpersonalities reunite with their own original qualities and her Self. By the time she returns home, she has started becoming her true loving, courageous, and wise Self.

In *The Fire Next Time*, James Baldwin writes of the battles between our self and our subpersonalities: "Love takes off the masks that we fear we cannot live without and know we cannot live within. I use the word 'love' here not merely in the personal sense but as a state of being, or a state of grace."

Families, too, along with their core identity, have subpersonalities, with the members playing different family parts, even several different parts or roles. These roles may be vehicles for their emotions or their feelings about their work, school, social, and even religious lives, and their placement in the family.

Cinderella's original family threesome—her mother, father, and herself—was loving, kind, and gentle. After her mother dies and her father remarries, she becomes part of a dysfunctional family, with a passive husband, an aggressive and cruel wife with two ugly and inadequate daughters, who serve, by contrast, to show how adequate and selfless our heroine is. The family is blended, made up of two different families that vie to maintain their original identities and rules in spite of the new members and circumstances.

Cinderella and her father are loving people who do not know how to respond to aggression, selfishness, and abuse. For their part, the stepmother and her daughters see Cinderella and her father as wimps and become even more demanding in the face of their passivity. At home the family subpersonality is polarized and has not synthesized the best aspects of a loving father and a powerful mother. At the ball, the stepmother and her two daughters fade while Cinderella shines, reversing the family roles at home.

Some of the roles family members play are basic and instinctual, born out of a need to survive, while others are more adaptable, changing as the family ages and changes. Some of these family roles mimic those of previous generations. Whether the family views the different roles members play as helpful or harmful, it is enriched and grows as it struggles with the diversity of its members' behaviors. As each member is a subpersonality of the family, integrating with or denying the family self, each family is a subpersonality of its society, capable of enriching or denying it. When we recognize this, we can begin to sense a universal Purpose and wisdom that help us accept the differences in ourselves, our families, and the wide world around us.

Families need structure and definite roles with clear boundaries that provide safety and respect, but the roles should not be so rigid as to preclude change.

Families can be so centralized and fused that a single person dominates, thwarting the individuality of each member. Conversely, families may be so decentralized, with no one assuming the executive, or parental, function, that the members feel isolated and disengaged from one another.

Physicist Gary Zukav, in his book *The Seat of the Soul*, describes a decentralized family as made of "splintered parts" that suffer as they seek to be reattached to the family soul. A family with no attachment to the energy of its soul has, he says, "no reference point, no connection, no mothership," and the conflict in its life is directly proportional to its distance from its soul. By contrast, when the family is in "full balance," it is connected to and reflects its soul.

Assagioli states that the more clearly aware we are of our subpersonalities, the more able we are to make choices and synthesize these parts of ourselves into a larger organic whole without repressing any of their useful aspects. He adds that the more we explore these parts of ourselves and stand back from them, the more we become our observing self, a function of the "I" that mediates between it and the subpersonalities.

THE WILSON FAMILY STORY

During the Great Depression of the 1930s, the young Wilson family had to manage with very little money. The mother became overly frugal to minimize what she spent. She bought only sale foods and used clothing, used the public library for books, walked rather than took any other form of transportation, relied on family members for free child care, and allowed no vacations or entertainment. Even after the Depression was over and the family started to be safe financially, she kept right on with these same behaviors, much to the embarrassment and discomfort of other family members. By the early 1950s, she had children in college, her husband had a car, and they had their own house. But she continued to buy second-hand clothes for her family and pass them down to the children. Although she had a college degree, she worked as a cook in a school cafeteria.

Her husband, while careful about money, adjusted to a higher income and felt no guilt about buying new shirts and shoes. He accepted his wife's frugality, didn't like its effects, but loved his wife nonetheless. One of her children identified with her frugal subpersonality, continued wearing second-hand clothes, and wouldn't allow herself many basic personal necessities. Instead of dis-identifying from the frugal family subpersonality, this daughter clung rigidly to it while her siblings could let it go and be more flexible with their spending patterns.

Later on, one of the siblings suffered a financial crisis. Although this child, like her father, was careful with money but not obsessively so, a corporate down-sizing left her unemployed for an extended period. She remembered her mother's ways of coping with very little money, and her family survived until her next job a year later. She coordinated and synthesized the financial lessons of both parents and modeled resilience for her children and future generations.

SUBPERSONALITY EXERCISES

Go back and look at the exercise in Chapter 2 that uses animals as a way of seeing family roles. These roles are subpersonalities. The exercises that follow will explore the different family subpersonalities in greater depth.

EXERCISE: FAMILY FAIRY TALES

Many fairy tales, myths, fables, and tall stories are useful for looking at personal, family, and societal roles.

Ask family members to choose a favorite fairy tale, myth, or fable and tell how the different people in the story are like parts of them. Then go one step further and have them discuss which family members play each role in the story.

For instance, in the case of "Jack and the Beanstalk," you could ask:

- Who in the family is Jack? Who is the mother? Who is the cow? Who is the man who sells Jack the magic beans? Is there anyone in the family who acts like magic beans? *[Pause for reflection or jotting down notes]*

Recall that Jack plants the beans, goes to sleep, and in the morning finds the beanstalk. Even though his mother fears for him, he chooses to risk climbing, or going into a higher consciousness, all the way to the giant's castle on the top.

Then ask:

- Who in the family is the giant? Who is the magic harp Jack finds in the castle? Who is the golden goose? Who is a golden egg? Who is the giant's wife? How are the characters in the castle on top of the beanstalk the same or different from the people on the ground? What does Jack learn by climbing the beanstalk?

As all identify their parts in whatever fairy tale the family chooses, have them tell how they feel physically, emotionally, and mentally about themselves, their family, and the world when they play this part.

EXERCISE: THE EVENING REVIEW FOR AN INDIVIDUAL

Psychosynthesist James Vargiu developed the evening review as a tool to allow you to become more aware of what roles you have played with others during the day. The exercise is usually done at the end of the day with journal and pen nearby.

Settle down and become calm and quiet. Relax your body, feelings, and mind, but stay alert. Allow yourself to get into the role of the observer, staying detached and non-critical as you review your day from morning to evening.

See your emotions as you review the day. Your aim is not to relive your experience, but to look for roles, patterns, and their meaning. Be sure to journal your answers. As you are reviewing, ask yourself:

- Which of your parts or roles were dominant during the day?
- What circumstances made a part emerge or withdraw?
- Did any of your parts come into conflict with each other?
- How much did your subpersonalities hinder or help what you wanted to do?
- Which ones were in the driver's seat in each incident?

Try and maintain your calm and objectivity and not get too emotionally involved in the day. When emotions come up, gently shift your focus back to that calm place you were in. Remain the observing self.

If you find yourself being too critical or judgmental of yourself or others, realize that the critic is a subpersonality, and step back and focus on the calm and the peace. It's a success to have discovered that critical or judgmental subpersonality. Ironically, this same critical subpersonality believes it wants your good, but it uses rigid means learned in your childhood to keep you in line and keep you from growing and changing. *[Pause to let go of the criticism.]*

As you begin to recognize and accept your subpersonalities, allow yourself to see how and when they were formed. Start by asking yourself how old your subpersonalities are and how long they have been part of how you react to others.

Allow yourself to see how some of your subpersonalities work together while others may want to dominate, how some are weak, some are strong, some want power, and some may be unable to express or accept love.

Once you are aware of your different subpersonalities, ask yourself how they work together or against one another.

Your goal in this exercise is to choose those subpersonalities that serve you best and allow you to express your true identity and adapt in any life situation. When you can do this, you can integrate, or synthesize, the needs and the qualities of all your subpersonalities into your whole person, choosing among them as needed.

EXERCISE: THE EVENING REVIEW FOR THE FAMILY

On another evening, after everyone has practiced the individual evening review, gather the family, seated, taking a few minutes for all to become calm and be ready with their journals. Remind everyone to observe their roles with a non-judgmental attitude. The purpose of the exercise is to see the roles, not to change them.

LEADER, *pausing frequently for journaling and discussion*:

"Who were you in the family today and when? Were you daughter or son, a husband or wife, a mother or father, sister or brother, a grandparent, an aunt or uncle?

"Do you see yourself as good or bad in any family role or with any one person in your family? Are you, for instance, a good son and a bad brother, or a good wife and a bad mother? Do these terms change from day to day?

"Did you feel you belonged, or were you a stranger? Were you the caregiver? The entertainer? The sick one? The angry person? The hero? The worker? The scapegoat? The lost one? The mascot?

"What happened in the family that had you take that role or roles? What happened in the family to make you not act yourself but react in one of the family roles?

"Who are you? What choices can you make to be who you are? What would happen in the family if you acted as you see yourself to be? Do you have a choice? Can you not act in the roles you usually play?

"What if the others in the family also chose to act as they really see themselves? How can you help them to be themselves?

"What roles did you, other family members, and your family as a whole play in society today? How do others perceive your family?"

Take time now for everyone to finish writing or drawing before you share with each other what you have written. As always, it is each person's choice how much or what they share. Discuss what roles the whole family shares with the extended family as well as the community.

THE INNER THEATER

Psychosynthesist Vivian King describes the personality as an "inner theater" with the Self as the Playwright, the "I" as the director, and the subpersonalities as the actors. The director's job is to get the actors to play by the script and the theme of the play. Some of the actors play to the audience and do not listen to the director, while others not only listen to the director but also acknowledge the Playwright as the author of the play. Among the actors are the stars, or the developed and polished aspects of ourselves, and players who represent our immature and weaker aspects and get in the play's way. In the wings are actors who have already played their scenes, those who have yet to come on stage, and a supporting cast of guest stars who represent our dreams and ideals. The guest stars include wise persons, spiritual figures, superheroes, mythological figures, great statesmen, heroes, angels, and others we admire.

EXERCISE: THE FAMILY INNER THEATER

Using paper strips, outline a stage on the floor. Together, as a family, choose a recent family incident or a subject under current discussion in the family. Have the family members most involved in the incident or decision be the actors on the stage. Choose one person to be the director, watching the action from the side of the stage, and to read the script. Family members not involved in the action of the play should take their places in the wings. Remember to set up one or two seats for those figures, real or imagined, that the family uses for guidance and wisdom.

LEADER:

"Actors, stand on the stage, in your places, and take time to be aware that there is a stage. Look around. In your imagination, do you see scenery? Look and see who is on this stage with you. Do you stand in one place or do you move about and talk to the other actors? Who is in the wings? Who is in the supporting cast for this family?

"Who do you imagine is in the audience? Neighbors? Friends? Teachers? Co-workers? Other relatives? Does the audience interact with the actors? Do you let audience members influence you? *[Pause and let the actors share what they see as their parts in the action of the play.]*

"Actors in the wings, why are you not on the stage? Will you soon be part of the action or have you not been asked to participate? Have you chosen to avoid the action?"

After setting the scene, the actors start the action. After they have played their roles for five or ten minutes, they stop and listen to the leader's directions for the director. The leader turns to the director and continues the script.

"Director, take a few deep breaths, step back from the stage in your mind and into your "I", staying disidentified from your emotional attachment to the action of the cast. Imagine that the Playwright has shown you the script and theme of this family and its Purpose for the world, and that the scene you just saw is one of many the family acts out in trying to understand the Playwright's Purpose in the script.

"Be aware, director, whether the family members involved in the action are also remembering the family Purpose or avoiding it out of fear of change or out of old perceptions and behaviors toward one another. Take a few more deep breaths, and imagine how the family members on stage might behave if they were identified with their own "I" and the family "I".

"You have questions to ask the actors to help them begin to understand the parts they are playing in this family. See if you can empower the actors to see what you are seeing. Remember, they are great pretenders, and your job is to bring them back into resonance with the theme of the play."

Now the director takes over, questioning the actors.

DIRECTOR'S QUESTIONS FOR THE ACTORS:

"When you are in this play, what name do you give yourself?

"How does the role you are playing in this play express itself physically? Are you tense? Relaxed? Sick? Healthy? Young? Old? Fat? Thin? Ugly? Beautiful?

"What are your emotions in this role? Do the other actors or audience affect your emotions in this role?

"What is your world view from this role? Are you able to think clearly, or do you feel confused, stuck, and without choice?

"As you experience this role, what are its needs? What does it want from the family? What does it want to have happen in this family?

"Does this role help or hinder this family's needs? Does it help the family harmonize with the family 'I'?

"Can you express your individuality in the family or does your family role decide who you are?

"Ask a member of the supporting cast for any wisdom or insight they may have."

After each actor has reflected on these questions, ask the actors to continue the action as it would happen if all were really getting their needs met and were in touch with their "I" and the family "I".

After the family has replayed the scene, the director asks the actors what insights they have experienced and what new behaviors they might want to incorporate into their lives. Talk about ways the family can practice the new behaviors and insights. Write them down. The family might even want to write a contract, spelling out how they will deal with each other when situations like this recur. Any time the family wants to stage a new scene, a different family member should be the director.

EXERCISE: HOW OTHERS SEE THE FAMILY

You will need pens, envelopes, slips of paper, and especially for the younger family members, art supplies. Give each person a set of envelopes and slips of paper. The envelopes are marked with topics such as Party, School, Vacation, Work, Home, Weddings, Funerals, Neighborhood, Sporting Events, Holidays, Doctor's Office, Visits to Relatives, and Place of Worship.

Also give each family member a copy of these questions:

- How do others perceive this family at this place or event?
- Does the family personality change depending upon where the family is and which members are present?
- If a camera followed this family around, what would it show when the family is together here?
- How do you feel about the family when you are here?

For each topic, have each person answer each of the four questions on a separate slip of paper and put it in the appropriate envelope. After all the envelopes are finished, collect and sort them by topic. Then topic by topic, have different family members read the answers aloud. Remember to receive each answer with acceptance.

For each topic, ask the family to think of one word or name that describes the family subpersonality in each circumstance. Put that word on the envelope. Now discuss and write on the envelope what this subpersonality needs and wants when in this situation. Do the same for all the envelopes. Save the envelopes for the next exercise.

EXERCISE: SHARING FAMILY QUALITITES

At a later meeting, seat the family in a circle with a chair in the middle to represent the family self, or "I". Have available a dozen or more different colored ribbons cut into approximately 18-inch lengths, a felt-point pen, and the envelopes from the previous meeting.

After distributing the envelopes to family members, ask a family member to read the family subpersonality name and its wants and needs on their envelope. Have all take a moment to identify with that subpersonality and ask themselves whether there is a quality that it is expressing or trying to express. A review of the list of qualities from Appendix II might be helpful here. Write down that quality on the envelope.

Now ask a family member to write the name of the quality from his or her envelope on a ribbon, take the ribbon, stand, and say:

"I am ___________(quality) in this family. I pass the ____________ (quality) of this family and its generations to you."

The person hands the ribbon on to another family member who rises, takes it, and says the same thing. The ribbon is handed on from family member to family member until each has spoken that quality aloud.

Then go to the next quality on the next envelope and repeat this process until all the family subpersonalities have been named and their qualities experienced by everyone. A greater sense of Purpose will become apparent to all family members.

Now ask family members with envelopes to take turns sitting in the center, or self, chair. Have each person now ask the self:

- What is the purpose of this family subpersonality?
- Is this subpersonality aware of its purpose?
- Can it choose to know and act out its purpose?

Write the purpose on the envelope. Continue this with each envelope. Ask all the members about how recognizing the family subpersonalities, qualities, and purpose helps the family be more resilient under stress.

Remember the Family Synthesis Questionnaire from Chapter 3 and the motto you chose for this family. What would happen if you took that family motto into each place or event? Does the motto now represent the family's qualities and Purpose in the world? If necessary, change the motto to better represent this Purpose.

Your family has explored the basics of Psychosynthesis theory and its applications to the family. In the next three chapters the family will learn how to develop and use its will to enact its purposes in the world.

FAMILY WILL

Brothers Leon and Michael Spinks were world champion boxers. Realizing that boxing was this African-American family's way to gain recognition, money, and respect, Cory, Leon's son, felt that the generations behind him plus his father's coaching would lead him to a world championship too. After winning the welterweight championship, he bulked up in hopes of winning the middleweight championship. But he lost. He felt he had lost for himself and the whole Spinks family.

However, in the tradition of the family, he tried again. He did not run away or hide. A Spinks didn't do that, but Cory was more humble this time. The next fight went twelve rounds. He stayed as though he could fight all night, upholding his family honor. A newspaper columnist said Spinks was "all willpower and soul and grit and resilience." He won and claimed the middleweight championship. The columnist added that the extra pounds Spinks had put on for the fight had all gone to his heart, which had lasted the fight and was as "good as reinforced steel."

This story illustrates the enormous power of family support, tradition, and determination. This same energy exists in every family, ready for all of its members to use to express who they are, their family "I". Assagioli calls this dynamic force and intention will.

By exploring and recognizing its "I", a family becomes aware of a force from it that urges the family toward action, choice, and expression of its authentic identity. The family can use will constructively to work toward wholeness and potential or destructively if it is ruled by the fears of its subpersonalities.

In his book *The Act of Will* Assagioli asks us to open ourselves to discovering that will exists as a function of the "I", that we have a will, and that we can align our will with Purpose. Through this we can recognize that whoever we are, wherever we go, we are will.

Assagioli identifies three aspects of the will that we can develop: strong will, skillful will, and good and loving will. He also acknowledges the Transpersonal Will of the Self and the Universal Will, or the Will of God, which we cannot change. Strong will, the most basic and familiar of these, is the sheer power we use to put our choices into action. Skillful will adds an element of strategy that helps us realize our goals most efficiently and effectively. These two aspects of will can help us, or we can use them to manipulate and harm others unless we accompany them with loving intent, or good will. When we use good and loving will to better mankind, we are manifesting the Will of the Self and Universal Will.

Every time we choose and act, or choose not to act, we are using will. When we feel stuck and don't act, even out of fear of hurting someone else, we are still making a choice. Ironically, it takes more energy to stay put, especially in adversity, than to move forward. Families, too, often feel it is easier to regress into past behaviors or do nothing than to stay active and aware of the family's priorities. However, as the family learns to exert and use its will, the initial effort, through discipline, becomes effortless. This discovery of family will awakens action, and a family finds a whole new sense of expansion and confidence.

Assagioli says that the simplest way to find will is through "determined action and struggle." As families struggle, act, and grow when faced with a problem, especially one that might mean change, they find that by meeting together and taking the time to connect with their "I" and will, they can feel supported and become more aware of their choices. They find the action coming out of struggling, choosing, and planning gives the family energy and life.

EXERCISE: THE FAMILY CROSSROADS

A traditional Psychosynthesis exercise called "The Crossroads" was designed to help us realize the importance of choice and will. This exercise is useful for individuals and families as they struggle with a goal, question, or decision.

As a family, choose a family decision, issue, or problem to explore. Make sure everyone has writing materials to note during the exercise their body sensations, images, feelings, and thoughts about the family, their roles, and the issue being explored. When the family comes together at the end of the exercise, it is important to share these experiences with each other.

LEADER:

"Sit back in your chair, and think about the problem or decision the family has chosen for this exercise. Think of an image or word that represents the family issue. You will take this with you on your journey.

"Now close your eyes and picture yourself and your family on a road, walking with your word or image in your mind. You are not trying to solve the issue; you are just walking with it.

"Ahead of you, you see a Y in the road, a crossroads. Choose your road and start walking, taking your word or image with you. *[Pause for reflection or writing each time you stop walking.]*

"Now stop wherever you are on your road and go back to the crossroads and see that there is a sign at the Y. It says, 'Both roads end in the same place.' What does this information mean to you?

Now keeping your image or word with you, imagine that you have become an observer, looking down on your family and the problem. Being up higher, you can see the crossroads. You can even see the two roads, what they look like, and how they meet in the end at the same place. Look down on your body, your family, and your image or word. You may begin to sense that there are more choices available to you and your family than you thought in the beginning. Come back down into your body, and choose a road, either one, and start walking again.

"Now stop again on the road you have chosen, and go back to the crossroads. Again see the sign. Again become the observer looking down on yourself, your family, and the roads. Choose to do this from an even higher place than before, above the observer, a place of peace, love, and Universal Will. Look down on yourself, your family, and the family issue. Experience a sense of Purpose and choice. Slowly leave this place and come down into yourself with the fullness of the experience. Now start walking on whichever road you choose. This time follow your road to the end.

"At your destination, see what has happened to your decision, image, or problem. You might have an insight about your image or word. It is enough that you experience a feeling of choice. Now come back into the family slowly. Everyone has been on a journey. Take a few minutes to write the story of your journey and your reactions to it."

Finally, allow each one to tell what they wish about their journey and what has happened to the family issue. Talk about what you have learned about your family and about family decision-making.

The crossroads exercise helps a family realize that even in difficult times, it has choices. Knowing this allows the family to strengthen its will to survive and use its will to adapt and be resilient. The way a family adapts, acts, and makes choices, even unconsciously, can be a way to express the family "I".

When a family expresses its "I", it gains energy and allows members to experience relationship with each other as well as with something greater than each member alone. We saw this in society when, in reaction to the terrorist attacks of Sept. 11, 2001, most Americans found a fellowship they hadn't known existed, and they found in each other an intense patriotism and sense of belonging. When challenged by adversity, the families of America showed strength of will to survive, resilience to endure, and a common purpose.

Family will can be found in quiet family moments when someone experiences an urge to express an insight about the family. The insight can be as simple as a suggestion to plan some sort of family activity, or it can be an idea of a new direction for the family. Being open to the urging and intention of the family "I" that can speak through any member allows the family to more fully experience its many different and rich choices.

EXERCISE: FAMILY CHOICES

Gather the family together at dinner time, breakfast time, or any time the family is not distracted by other activities. Talk about the choices the family will make for the coming day. Own the choices by saying "I choose to____" or "We choose to _______." To get and keep the discussion going, ask questions like:

- What are we going to eat? Who is going to fix the food?
- What activities are we going to do? At work? At school?
- What chores need to be done at home and who is going to do them?
- When are we going to do our activities? How do we help or hinder each other in using our time?
- What will we do for recreation? TV? Games? Reading? Sports?
- What other choices will each family member make today that will affect the family? What decisions will we make today that will affect tomorrow? What decisions will we make today that will affect next year?
- What choices will we make about money today?
- What choices will we make about which people we talk to in the family? About showing affection and love in the family?

The family may be planning a vacation. As all family members get involved with the choice and can give their views and feel accepted for their reasons for or against the vacation, the choices in the decision become clearer. As the family focuses on the decision, the energy of their collective will increases. This also occurs when one member is making a choice, tells the family, and feels the family's supportive energy while making a decision and choosing to act.

STRONG WILL

When most people think of as will, they think of what Assagioli describes as strong will. Strong will is often exhibited as determination, discipline, decision-making, and decision-keeping. Many see strong will as the stubbornness of the "strong-willed" child. However, it sometimes takes strength of will and stubbornness to survive in times of great adversity such as war and disease.

As a child, Theodore Roosevelt was so incapacitated by asthma that he had to be home-schooled until he left for college. The family constantly rushed him from seaside resorts to mountain cabins to help him breathe. He was not expected to survive his childhood. Yet he did. Before he set out for college, his father told him that he must become a strong man and embrace life through vigorous exercise. Resolved to make himself stronger, Teddy, as he was often called, started on a life of self-determination, strong will, and vigor with daily exercise, sports, outdoor activity, and adventure. He stated in an autobiography that he made an ideal of fearlessness and practiced every day to achieve it, even if it meant risking injury or his life.

Roosevelt not only made decisions; he followed through on them. But for many of us follow-through does not come easily. Whether we make a personal decision to lose weight or stop smoking or a family decision to have weekly meetings, eliminate TV on weekdays so that homework gets done, or do chores on Saturday mornings, the needed discipline sometimes feels burdensome. All family members have to remember that they chose to participate in the decision, and they must be willing to support and seek support from other family members as all struggle to follow through. Each time a person is aware of following through on a choice, the strength of the choice increases.

Some see strong will as rigid and determined, inflexible and joyless, only strength. This is evident when one family member has the my-way-or-the-highway attitude, taking on strong will for the entire family, or when undisciplined children get everything they want. Although these are examples of strong will and its power, the family can use it for its good as well as its harm.

EXERCISE: USING STRONG FAMILY WILL TO CHANGE BEHAVIOR

Set a time for a family meeting, a task of will all of its own. Ask each member to bring a list of things about the family they want to keep and things they want to change. In a non-judgmental atmosphere, also requiring strong will, ask each person to read aloud his or her list.

Ask one person be the secretary and collate the lists on a large piece of paper, backboard, or flip chart. Some items may be the same for several family members and some different. As you read the lists, notice what items the family agrees on. Then, as a family, pick one item that the family might want to change.

Find a simple word, phrase, or sentence that describes this item, and write it on cards or slips paper that you will later put on the refrigerator or mirrors so that each family member can be reminded about what they wish to change. The following examples are too broad and too difficult to achieve, as are most statements including "always" and "never":

- "I will show love to everyone."
- "I will always be on time."
- "I will never be late."
- "I will never fight with anyone."
- "I will always do my chores."

The following examples are likely to bring more success:

- "I will give everyone a smile in the morning."
- "I will say hello to everyone when I get home."
- "I will be on-time for ___________." Fill in the blank with something like "carpool," "breakfast," "dinner," "school," or "work."

- "I will listen to what the other person has to say before I argue with them."
- "I will try to make my bed each morning."
- "This family will set aside time each night to say 'goodnight' to each other and give each other a hug."

Ask all family members if they can agree to this change and if they will use their own strong will to live it out. It is important that everyone—adults and children—agree and be able to enter into this new way of acting and take personal responsibility for it.

Set up another family meeting in a week or two and see how successful each person has been. Ask each how much strong will it took to do this activity. Did it seem effortless, or did it need lots of choice and strength? Was it too hard? If so, the statement may not have been specific enough and so may need to be broken down into more manageable components. Maybe, for instance, being on time requires an alarm or a watch. However, the family is growing by helping all members experience their own strong will. Again, it is important to support each other and not criticize failures, which also takes strong will.

EXERCISE: USING THE FAMILY SYNTHESIS QUESTIONNAIRE

Question 17 in the Family Synthesis Questionnaire asked you about strength of will in your family's different generations. Read this again. Had you recognized will in the family before? How did your family use strength of will in past generations? What was the dominant strength of your family and how did it show everyone the self or identity of this family?

Examples are often found in family moves, country to country, home to home, job to job. Families also show their strength to survive when they have very little money and yet save to educate a child, buy a house, or adopt children from other cultures. In today's world, families are often stressed when members marry outside their religion or race, choose to live at great distances, or select careers that aren't family-approved.

What challenges did your family of origin face and how did they use strong will to survive?

The next chapter will build on what your family has learned here by showing you how to temper your will and use it skillfully to explore your choices and act on them.

SKILLFUL FAMILY WILL

Some cultures, families, and individuals are known for their strong will. Psychoanalyst Erik Erickson tells how, in some Native American cultures, mothers purposefully slap their sons when breast-feeding them to encourage them to be aggressive, fearless, determined fighters. President Theodore Roosevelt is another example. But, unable to discipline his obsessive desire to prove himself fearless and powerful, he put himself in unnecessarily dangerous situations. He needed to learn how to marshal personal skills other than sheer strength when confronted with a crisis.

As a family, the Marches of Louisa May Alcott's novel *Little Women* had not only developed strong will to survive, but something more. The story takes place in Massachusetts during the Civil War. The family is in crisis because Mr. March, the father, has gone to fight, leaving Mrs. March and four daughters with no means of support. They are so poor that they decide to celebrate Christmas without presents.

The book starts with the four girls commiserating with each other about their situation, arguing and trying to decide what they might be able to buy for themselves anyway. Then, by suggesting that they buy something for their mother instead, Beth turns their angry feelings into creative and loving feelings for Mrs. March. Later that day, Jo helps make time fly by suggesting that they make a game of an uninteresting sewing project. And so the story of the Marches begins by showing how they are learning to help one another deal with the mundane and sometimes sad and frightening aspects of life, adding to their strong will to survive a quality Assagioli describes as skillful will.

Skillful will moderates strong will by giving us a range of abilities and choices to reach goals. Assagioli illustrates skillful will with a star diagram, each of its six points showing a function, or element, of our psyche that we can use skillfully with our will.

These six functions—emotion/feeling, intuition, thought, imagination, impulse/desire, and sensation—exist in all of us. We often use them mechanically, without insight or discipline, but we can learn to influence, govern and direct them. We have choice.

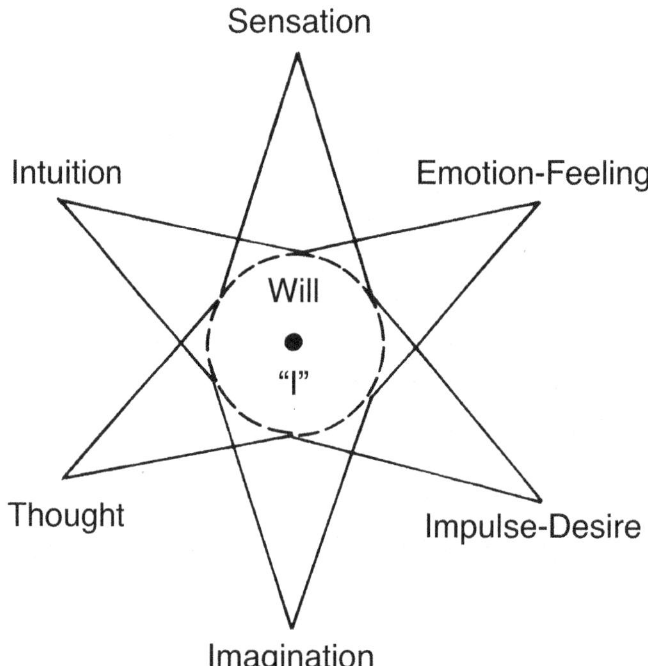

EXERCISE: THE INDIVIDUAL STAR DIAGRAM

In order to do this exercise, you will need to keep at hand a copy of the star diagram so that you can refer to it.

Think of a problem, something you would like to understand or do better, something about yourself that you might want to change. Whatever idea first comes to mind, accept and use for the exercise. Write it down. You can do this exercise seated and imagining yourself through the different functions of the star diagram, or you can stand and physically move through the exercise. Take a few minutes to center before you begin.

See yourself in the center of the star, your "I." See the six functions or talents that are there for you to use to explore and clarify the problem you are working on. Visualize from this center the "I" energy, which propels you forward and uses each of the six different functions to work with you on any issue.

Start with any function you like and step into it. Feel the energy of choosing, while still connected to your center. As you look at your problem through this function, let it tell you about itself and you and how it can help you with your problem. Fully listen and experience the creativity of this function in dealing with your problem. Ask it what is really important about your problem, what needs to happen, what stops you, and what qualities you may need to develop to solve the problem. Go back to your seat, breathe deeply, and write down what you learned from this function.

Repeat this process with each of the six functions. Each time go to the center, dis-identify with the function you had just experienced, then step into and identify with a new function, each time asking it to inspire you with more understanding about your problem. Write down your answers or understandings as you go though all the functions.

In the sensation/body element, physically experience your problem in the world around it. Use the other functions to understand your desires, thoughts, and feelings about it. Allow your intuition and imagination to communicate creative choices to you. Even if you are uncomfortable with intuition and imagination, they can reach you though your thoughts, feelings, desires, and sensations. Assagioli says some intuitions are inspirations from the Higher Self urging us to action for our greater good. For now, it is enough just to experience that you have intuition and imagination.

Allow yourself to marvel at all the resources you have explored. See how your process of choosing to explore each function has made you feel more in control and yet not controlling. See how free and thankful you feel. Again center and allow energy, peace, and freedom to be there for you.

You have used your skillful will to look at your problem from your center, directing your energy out through the different functions. Now you can use it to help you execute any solutions you may have discovered. As you do this, remember to stay centered, and to use all the functions, not just those that come easiest to you.

EXERCISE: THE FAMILY STAR DIAGRAM

We can illustrate using skillful will to explore alternatives, set goals, and take action by having different family members become the different will functions from the star diagram while exploring a family issue.

Before you start the exercise, decide as a family what issue you want to look at. It may be something as simple as vacation or school plans. It may deal with the family's interaction with extended family members, neighbors, or the community, or it may be about a world issue. It may also be about a potential quality that the family wants to express. The family needs to agree on the issue and talk about their individual goals, intentions, and motivations about it.

As in other exercises, have journaling materials available and plenty of uninterrupted time. On each of six letter-size pieces of paper write one of the functions of will. Decide where the family "I" is going to be in the room and arrange the pieces of paper around it, like rays of the star.

Start with everyone moving to the family "I", or center. You can use chairs in a circle, facing out, or you can stand together.

LEADER:

"Now that we are all together, take time to quiet and become aware of the family center, the family 'I'. Someone please say what the family issue is that we want to understand today. Now, each person get up, and in your own time, move from the center into one of the six functions, the function where you feel most comfortable in the family.

"Look around the room and see: Who is the thinker for the family? Who is the family imagination? Who is the family intuition? Who expresses the family feelings and emotion? Who represents the physical for the family? Who represents its impulses and desires?

"Notice where everyone is standing and if there is more than one person on some functions and none on others:

- "Does the family think and not feel?
- "Does the family feel and not think?
- "Are intuition and imagination allowed in this family?
- "When a member represents the physical of the family, are they sick or healthy?
- "Do one or more members feel that they actually represent more than one element?

"From the vantage point of the function you have chosen, fully experience the family issue and see what insights about it come up. Ask your function what is really important about this family issue, what needs to happen, what gets in the way, and what qualities the family may have to develop to solve the issue. Use your skillful will and choose to write or draw about the experience of the family issue from the function you are in." *[Pause for everyone to write or draw.]*

"Now go back into the family center and quiet. Let go of the issue and the will functions, and just allow the family 'I' to refocus everyone on the family Purpose. Sit in the light and the peace, the sense of who this family deeply is. From this deeper place, look out on the functions and realize that from the view of the Self, all functions are useful and important, and that you can use will skillfully to direct and execute the family's choices."

Now go back to the regular family seating and talk together about the original issue and what you found out from your function and from the center. Using the insights from each person, clarify the issue and decide what action you want take.

Whenever the family is together, members may have a thought, feeling, desire, sensation, image, or intuition they want to share. It's important for the family to encourage all ideas, develop the discipline to receive them in a non-judgmental way, and choose whether to act on them. The action and skill are in the choosing, not just in the receiving. When the family uses its imagination to see the limitations, drawbacks, and advantages of any idea, it generates momentum toward change.

PSYCHOLOGICAL LAWS OF WILL

In the exercises in the disidentification chapter, you observed your body, feelings, and thoughts before centering on your experience of your self. Will, the energy that comes from the "I", can use these same sensations and thoughts to build habits and even subpersonalities. Any life experience that creates a physical, emotional, and mental response can, with repetition, become a habitual, automatic, and even unconscious way of perceiving reality. The more it is repeated, the greater the likelihood that it will become habitual. The resulting habits can work against our goals, or we can consciously use our will to build the habits we want. It's our choice.

Remember the star diagram and its six functions. With skillful family will, we can use those functions to become aware of old family habits and build new ones by creating mental images of the physical performance of a task, seeing how these images affect us emotionally, and how, by repetition, the physical, emotional, and mental responses become habitual.

If, for example, the family would like everyone to make their bed, the family must first have an image of what a made bed looks like, then of the physical action of making a bed, and an image of when this would occur, and so on. The fuller and more explicitly physical the image is, the greater the chance that the beds will actually get made.

Or suppose the family wants to work on promptness. First, all would imagine what they would physically have to do to realize their goal. Then they would explore their emotions about promptness and all its advantages and disadvantages for them. Finally, they would decide on the choices each person could make and the actions they would repeat to acquire the habit of being on time.

Like actors, even before we memorize our lines, we get into a role first by visualizing how it moves, feels, and acts. The more we practice and live our part, the more intense its experience becomes. If the part reflects who we are, our authentic self, we have a greater chance of experiencing will.

EXERCISE: ROLE PLAYING HABITS

Before gathering together, ask family members to decide on a family habit, exhibited either by the entire family or certain members, that they would like to explore.

Begin the meeting with family members writing their names on scraps of paper and putting them in a bowl. Allow each person time to tell their intellectual, emotional, and physical experiences of how they play their parts in the habit. They should describe only their own, not other people's, experience.

After all have shared their experiences, family members trade places with each other. Draw names from the bowl to see who each person will play. Give everyone a few minutes to physically and emotionally prepare their role. Now, imagining that the habit has come up, have the family act out a scene about it, all assuming their assigned roles. After playing the scene, everyone sits back down, centers, and takes a few minutes to write and talk about what happened.

Since much of our behavior is unconscious and habitual, it often takes will and courage to face up to our actions, motivations, and habits. If a family member wants to change a habit, the family needs to support that person non-judgmentally. Family members also need support in discovering the positive and negative habits they display with people outside the family, in their jobs and schools.

It is important to see how many of these habitual behaviors are not just reactions to the present but come out of past experiences, even experiences in past generations. More and more psychologists and scientists are discussing generational memories and inherited attitudes, talents, and problems. Even work with DNA and gene mapping asks:

- How much of us is determined by our heredity?
- Is there some sort of family inheritance of attitudes and ways of interacting with the world? Do we inherit our family's problems and Purpose?
- Does each of us choose, from the family we are in, to repeat old assumptions, hurts, hopes, and desires and to act them out? If so, why?

Family Synthesis contends that we repeat old dysfunctional familial hurts and assumptions until a family member learns to heal them by choosing to behave differently. Therefore, it behooves the current generation to examine these old wounds and see if we can learn from them.

EXERCISE: HEALING THE GENERATIONS

Have the family sit comfortably, quietly, and individually peaceful and centered, inviting in the family Self.

LEADER:

"As a family let's decide on an issue, feeling, or problem that we recognize has been going on for a long time in the family. *[Pause for discussion.]*

"Go to your inner place of peace and ask the family Self to be a guide, a helping spirit, to help us with this issue. Take time to experience this issue in your body.

"Think of when you first felt or experienced this family problem. See what your feelings were. If seeing the origins of the problem makes you afraid, ask the Self to stay at your side.

"Now reach inside yourself where the old feeling or experience is strongest, and see what image or shape it takes. What does it look like?

"Now ask your image or shape what the family needed at that past time. In your heart of hearts, see what the family needed but didn't get.

"As you understand that family need, go back to your inner place of peace and allow a new symbol or image to emerge for the family issue.

"Ask the old symbol to allow the new symbol to absorb its energies and its problems. Take time to let this happen. Using your imagination, talk to the new symbol and listen to what it says about your family problem. Ask for its advice and give it an assignment to help with the family issue and complete it in the next twelve to twenty-four hours. *[Pause for reflection and writing.]*

"Take your new symbol back to your place of peace and give it a place of honor.

"Who in your family's past generations could benefit from this new symbol? Can you see them? Try to see their old symbol for themselves and their problem.

"Ask them if this problem occurred in generations before them. Now see how this problem has come down through the generations into your family now.

"Ask the old generational symbol to be willing to be absorbed by your new symbol. As it allows itself to transform, let it heal the whole line of generations, past, present, and future.

"Slowly come back into the present and take time to write about your journey."

After you have done this, and everyone has had a chance to inwardly reflect, talk about what you have learned from the exercise. Some may wish to tell more than others.

Then talk about what other characteristics you now see as inherited or carried down through the family generations. Some may be positive and useful, and some may burden the family or hold it back. Remember each generation's job is to try to turn any characteristic into an effective tool for the family to grow and express itself to the world.

TECHNIQUES OF SKILLFUL WILL

Since old habits have power, even in families, skillful will techniques can help families become aware of and change ingrained habits. The techniques Assagioli describes for doing this are substitution, evocative words, acting-as-if, and the ideal model.

EXERCISE: SUBSTITUTION TECHNIQUE

Substitution takes the energy or interest from one habit and invests it into another. This is not a case of ignoring the unwanted habit, which just gives it more power and makes it more unconscious, but of substituting one image of equal power or interest for the original.

This technique is often used in hypnosis and acupuncture. Whether we focus our attention on a peaceful place or throbbing needles, we gain release from the pain of dentistry, childbirth, or old injuries. It's all a matter of substituting one image or experience for another.

Some of these same techniques are being used in the treatment of depression. Psychiatrist David Burns, in his book, *Feeling Good*, shows us how. He gives examples of self-defeating statements such as:

- "I can't ___________."
- "I'm a jerk."
- "Nobody loves me."
- "I'm not good enough."

He asks readers to substitute statements like to

- "I can ____________."
- "I am capable."
- "I am smart."
- "I am lovable."

To make us aware of negative self-statements, he recommends using a golf counter to count them or a rubber band on the wrist that we snap every time that we make them. We then immediately substitute a positive self-statement. For procrastinators, he suggests changing "I can't do this whole project" to "I can do this piece of it."

According to Assagioli we can also use substitution to neutralize negative environmental influences such as violence, hatred, and greed. He suggests not ignoring but taking care not to feed these poisons. By withholding our attention from violent and overtly sexual movies, television shows, and music, we won't contribute to the inherent psychological pollution in them, and we can cultivate in ourselves nonviolence, courage, moderation, joy, and love.

From Burns and Assagioli, families can learn that the more they focus their attention on their dysfunctional habits, the more those habits will grow. Similarly, the more they focus on their talents and capabilities, the more those will grow.

First, family members have to be aware that a habit is dysfunctional and that they want change. After recognizing this, a family can have a meeting and discuss behaviors, statements, and images that are problematic and what could be substituted for them.

Little Sarah was sucking her thumb, and she and her family wanted her to stop. They suggested that if she did, they would reward her with a visit to a theme park. Every time Sarah wanted to suck her thumb, she thought of the theme park. Her desire to go to the park overcame her desire for her thumb. The substitution worked.

Substitution can be taken to extreme, causing denial, dissociation from reality, and isolation from the world. This is especially true when a family has been through a trauma such as divorce, death, sickness, war, or abuse, whether sudden or long-standing. Any of these severe situations provides the family an excellent opportunity to use substitution to encourage one another, but the goal and what is substituted need to be realistic and not overly ambitious.

EXERCISE: EVOCATIVE WORDS

Words and their meaning to us affect our sense of well-being, either negatively or positively. They produce in us states of mind and physical being and prompt us to act in ways that can be helpful or hurtful to us. In families certain words show encouragement and help support everyone in moving ahead.

Gather the family together, seating everyone comfortably, and allowing time for everyone to quiet and center.

LEADER:

"Imagine a sphere of light over your head. Ask the light for a word or brief phrase that the family can use for encouragement. The word or phrase may describe a quality that the family wants for itself and one another such as patience, service, humor, truthfulness, courage, faith, gratitude, love, and so on. For more suggestions see Appendix I or find your own quality word or phrase for the family.

"Each person, in turn, say aloud the word or phrase the light has given you. Everyone write down the word or phrase you have heard. When we have each written our quality, let's take time to share what we have written.

"Now, everyone take a few moments to reflect on all the words you have heard and allow your mind to evoke a single word or phrase that encompasses all the others.

"Let's share again these single words and phrases with each other. Is there one in particular that evokes for all of us the encouragement and support we need from each other? Let's agree together on the one word or phrase so that we can see it and use it all this next week. If two words or phrases seem equally important, let's do one this week, and try the other next week."

Post the chosen word or phrase strategically around the house where everyone can see it during the day—on refrigerators and bathroom mirrors, for instance. Repeat the word or phrase several times a day to yourselves and be aware of what thoughts and feelings it evokes. After several days, share with one another your different experiences.

Keep the word or phrase posted, repeat it, and talk about it from time to time. When a family problem comes up, call a meeting, and, to be open to a solution, speak the encouraging word or phrase aloud together. Then talk about the problem.

EXERCISE: ACTING-AS-IF TECHNIQUE

With this technique, family members act as if they already have a particular ability or quality they want, and this helps them internalize it in their bodies, thoughts, and emotions. If, for instance, they want patience, they start by talking about it and how they would act it out. For example, they could discuss how they will behave when a visiting relative with Alzheimer's may be trying everyone's patience. They decide in advance how to control their impatience and show her kindness and gentleness.

During her visit, family members can help each other by noticing and remarking on their acts of patience with the visitor and each other. "I saw how patient you were with Aunt Helen when she didn't recognize you," someone might say. The more the family members make comments like this, the more they affirm and encourage patience in each other.

Family members can recognize other qualities they are trying to acquire in the same way. For example:

- "I saw how kind you were with the dog."
- "I understand how thoughtful you were with your fellow employee today."
- "You were so helpful with your brother and his homework."
- "Thanks for being responsible and taking out the garbage without being asked."

Individual family members also need to reinforce desired qualities in themselves by being aware when they exhibit them and giving themselves credit.

Acting-as-if can see people through dreadful danger. I remembering hearing of two teen-aged girls, strangers to each other, who were abducted at gun point and thrown into the back of the abductor's van. By acting as if they had courage, they helped each other undo their restraints. When the van slowed for a stop, they opened the rear door, fell out, and started running. Afterwards, they told how terrified they were but said that by acting calm and in charge, they were able to plot their escape.

Acting-as-if does not deny reality or make problems go away. Denial is a defense against reality, a mechanism of fear. But once we accept reality and our problems, acting-as-if can use skillful will to correct them.

EXERCISE: THE IDEAL MODEL

Here is a way for a family to better understand who they are and their yearnings to be all they can be. The exercise uses the imagination aspect of skillful will, along with evocative words and acting-as-if.

At a family meeting, be sure everyone has paper and pencil. Appoint someone to be a recorder of everyone's answers, later putting them together in a summary.

LEADER:

"On your sheet of paper, write the characteristics of the family as we are now. *[Pause for writing after each instruction.]*

"Now write down the characteristics you would like the family to have.

"Write how you would like this family to appear to others.

"Write about how you think others see us now.

"How do you think others would like us to be? Write this down.

"How would you like us to behave with each other? Feel about each other? Think about each other? Describe the family you think we can become. Write your answers down.

"Pass all of your answers to the recorder."

The recorder reads all the answers aloud.

"Now that you have heard everyone's answers to all the questions, what do you think are the most realistic and desirable characteristics for this family to aspire to?" *[Pause for discussion.]*

"Visualize yourself with these qualities. How would you act in the family with these qualities? Use your will to see the choices you might make in your behavior with family members. Visualize different roles or circumstances where you could apply these qualities.

"Think of some words that evoke these qualities. Write the words down and share them with each other. Decide as a family would you would like to do to remember these words."

In the next chapter, you will learn the importance of cultivating the elements of love and goodness with will.

FAMILY GOOD AND LOVING WILL

Many people, especially children, believe that families come from love relatioships. Not all families do. But because love and a desire for goodness need to be cultivated, they can be acts of will. A decision to love and view someone else with goodness is a daily, often hourly choice, especially when that someone has hurt you and made you angry.

Similarly, many families decide to act with goodness toward others and the environment. They choose to recycle, compost, use environmentally friendly products, and not litter. What other choices can your family make to show goodness to the environment? In a family meeting or at a dinner discuss what actions your family wants to take to realize that we all have responsibility for where we live.

Remember any choice and action you make and follow through on strengthens the will.

Goodness to others means taking responsibility to view relationships with love rather than fear and loathing. The process begins with loving ourselves, who we were created to be, our intrinsic "I", and experiencing gratitude to the Universe for our creation. Often we let love flow through us to the outer world but will not let others love us back because we think it would be egotistical to accept their love and admiration. What we do not realize is how shutting out others' love hurts them as much as us.

As writer James Baldwin says, "Love is so desperately sought and so cunningly avoided. Love takes off the masks that we fear we cannot live without and know we cannot live within." It takes an act of will, courage, and grace, to step beyond our subpersonalities and risk loving. All myths and fairy tales are about this quest.

EXERCISE: WILLING TO LOVE

Pair family members off so that two people are facing each other.

LEADER:

"Each person take a turn saying to your partner, 'I love you but you do not love me.' You can use your hands or body to show giving out love and then refusing love, or you can just use the words.

"Discuss with your partner how this feels. Each of you will notice how bad it feels to have the other person not recognize your love. *[Pause for reflection]*

"Now face each other and say, 'I love you and you love me.' That may feel strange at first, but as you do this to each other, the person being recognized as loving starts to feel better.

"Come back together as a family. Each one tell your experience of being recognized as loving and not loving. *[Pause for discussion]*

"Each of you make a choice that during the next week you will silently say to each person you meet, 'I love you and you love me.' Come back to the family at the end of the week and share your experiences with each other."

This exercise teaches that when we don't recognize that someone is capable of loving us, we are also not recognizing that they are a Self. St. Francis knew this. He called every living thing, not just human beings, "brother" or "sister," assuming all were capable of responding with love. Try spending some time to consciously follow his example and experience the fruit of this perspective.

When we treat others with goodness and love, we are choosing to empathize with them and use our will to understand them and accept their faults and values just as we must accept our own. In psychotherapy, as people accept themselves and become conscious of all of their different aspects, they also are able to experience better relationships with others. One of the reasons so many of us have trouble with "I love you and you love me" is that we feel so bad about ourselves, we do not want others to notice us. This is the ultimate selfishness, being so involved with ourselves that we cannot be involved with others. This leads to depression, and the intense despair causes us to build a wall between us and everyone else. Yet behind it we feel anger, fear, discouragement, stress, and low self-esteem.

EXERCISE: WILL AND THE FAMILY WALL OF FEAR

Have paper and pen or pencil available for each person to draw or describe their wall and to write about their experience. Family members can be seated for the exercise.

LEADER:

"Each of us has experienced putting up a wall between us and others to, we believe, protect us from hurts. We start building our wall when we are very young, usually when someone hurts our feelings or doesn't understand us. We build this wall brick by brick, stone by stone, believing it protects us. The wall can come between each of us in the family and between the family and the outside world, eventually isolating us from each other and other people.

"Feel what it is like to be inside your wall. Realize that whatever it is like, even if it is dark and scary or you feel stuck, it is the wall that is keeping you here.

"Allow yourself to get close enough to the wall to see and feel what it is made of. Rocks? Bricks? Steel? Gluey stuff you can't pass through? Is it like a fence? How high is it? Do you feel as if you are in a tower on the wall? Walls are different for different people. No matter what they are made of, they isolate you.

"Now everyone draw or write about your wall. *[Pause for writing]*

"Now, in turn, each of you tell what material your wall is made of. Remember, there is no right or wrong answer. *[Pause for each to speak]*

"Are any you aware of walls between us in this family? Is there a family wall between us and others outside the family? Is it tall and rigid? Is it permeable or solid? What is it made of and how does it keep others out? How does it feel behind the family wall? *[Pause for discussion]*

"Go back to looking at your own wall and see the word 'FEAR' written in large letters on it. All walls, whether between individuals or families, are made of fear.

"You and the family are still behind the wall. Although you may feel angry and even depressed, realize that you and the family stay because it feels safer and more familiar here than outside. However, if you or anyone in the family feels bad enough, you may decide to risk moving beyond the wall of fear. See if you can choose to do that now.

"Say 'I am *willing* to move beyond this wall.' Keep saying these words as you get closer to your wall. Put your hand on it and see how it feels. Can you see a way to get beyond your wall? Is there a door? A gate? A window? Will you need a shovel? A ladder? A rope? A helicopter? A jack-hammer? Some other tool to help you? Is there some way you can help each other?

"The wall is going to resist anyone getting beyond it. It is going to tell you how much you need it and not to be a fool and go outside. It is very seductive in trying to keep you inside.

"Keep saying 'I am *willing* to get beyond this wall.' Is it too frightening? Do you need a wise person with you? Ask yourself for that wise person to help you and your family. Choose to go beyond the wall."

"If you are too frightened or resistant, it's all right to stop here and come back later. For those who want to go on, now is the time to go through your wall. Raise your hand when you are through. *[Pause until all have raised their hands]*

"Now that you are beyond your wall, look around and see where you are. Find a path or road and start walking on it.

"Ahead you will see someone waiting for you. Walk up and tell this person about yourself, your family, and your journey here, and let this person tell you about himself or herself. Ask him or her any question about your life, your family, your next step, and where you and the family are going. *[Pause for reflection]*

"Start walking again, taking your friend's hand. Realize that this person and you are becoming one person, looking out of your eyes and sharing your thoughts, feelings, and body. Experience the loving and peaceful relationship you now share. Your friend will not leave you and can be called on whenever you want or when anyone in the family needs wisdom.

"The wall is now behind the family. Can any of you get seduced by the wall again? Of course, but now each of you can count on your friend who is really your self, your 'I', and ever in you. You can also count on the family Self. Remember the road and this experience, and you will get beyond the wall again. It is all in your choosing and willing. Take a few minutes to write of your experience with the wall and your self." *[Pause to write, and then have everyone share their experiences.]*

It is important to understand the difference between walls and boundaries, which may seem the same since both were designed to keep us safe. Particularly for individuals, walls are built on fear and may become ways of life. Many families put up walls around certain topics they consider too dangerous or fearful to discuss.

Boundaries, on the other hand, are the physical, emotional, and psychological limits we choose to put on our interactions with others and the world. They are unseen lines between individuals within the family, the family and extended family members, and the family and the community. They are not only physical but also psychological distances. In families with poor emotional boundaries, members unconsciously shoulder responsibility for other family members' feelings, thoughts, and even physical well-being.

Assagioli writes about love and will as separate, each with its own aspects, yet with an inseparable relationship to each other. He describes the different types of love as maternal, paternal, fraternal, sexual, altruistic, humanitarian, and the love of God. Some loves come spontaneously; others require strength of choice and will, balanced by goodness and skill. Some families seem to exhibit more will than love, or vice versa. Some are more emotional, warm, and spontaneous; others are more volitional, seemingly cold and unfeeling. All families need both the emotional and the volitional, both love and will, and they need to strengthen whichever aspect is weaker. As family members become aware of this, their daily decisions will tell whether they are balancing love and will.

Most important to Assagioli is using good will toward each other and, in the interest of world peace, to the world at large. He noted that the preamble to the constitution of UNESCO states that wars begin in the minds of men, so it is in the minds of men that peace must be constructed. He added that the most effective way to change minds, both individual and collective, is the constant application of good will, which automatically excludes violent conflicts and war.

SYNTHESIS OF OPPOSITES

As individuals, families, and societies, we sometimes break up into factions that take starkly opposite sides of issues. As individuals, we may see our choices as between pleasure and pain, between our desires and the consequences of them. We vacillate between feeling loved and judged, or even hated, between attraction and repulsion. We have confidence or we are afraid; we feel good or we are depressed. At work we are in charge or we are slaves. We see the world in black or white, very good or very bad, the best or the worst.

This either-or thinking can also dominate families. From the time we are very young, parents and grandparents may teach us their view of the world as either full of possibilities or limiting us to the socio-economic situation to which we were born. We also inherit ideas of how parents should discipline children and what expectations parents should have for their children's careers, educations, and relationships. In some families, the expectations are positive and generous, in others rigid and onerous. Marriages encourage intimacy and affection or are distant and non-physical. We hold fast to family traditions or we rebel against the old ways. Our ideals inspire or oppress us.

As societies, we see no neutral countries, only other nations that are either our enemies or allies, democracies or dictatorships. Some people vote straight Republican or Democratic tickets, believing independents have no morals or backbone.

Either-or thinking is a coping mechanism. People who continue to see themselves and the world in black-or-white terms are rigid, fragile, and unable to cope with change. Openness to hearing others' opinions, recognizing other ways of coping, and seeing the gray in life allows people to change, adjust, and be resilient.

Compromise is crucial. In labor talks and international negotiations, it allows both sides to be heard and seek some sort of middle ground that incorporates something of both. It is a balancing of opposites, an example of both-and rather than either-or thinking. But there is a higher unity, often spiritual, beyond just compromise or the balancing of opposites. It incorporates both poles of a situation but transcends them into a new way of thinking and doing. This is synthesis.

Assagioli uses triangle diagrams to illustrate this point. At the two bases are examples of opposite attitudes, with a center point illustrating compromise between them and, above them, the synthesis. For example:

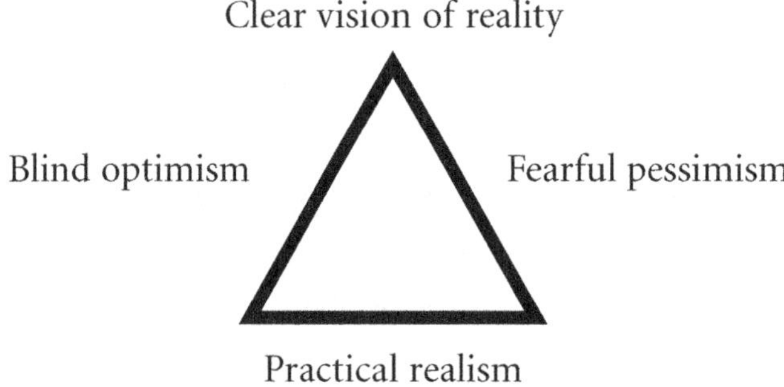

Benevolent understanding

Sympathy

Antipathy

Indifference

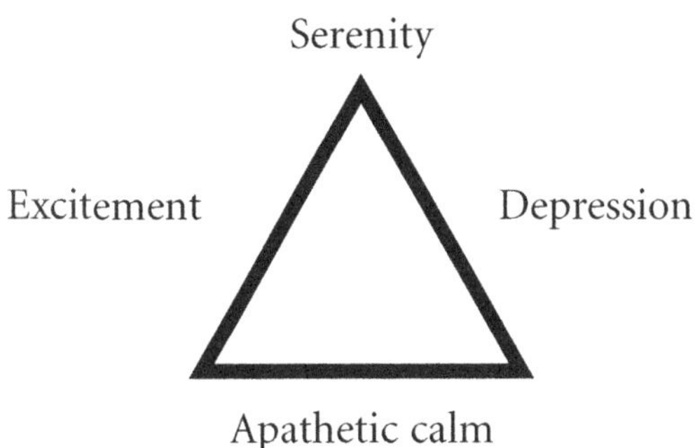
Serenity
Excitement
Depression
Apathetic calm

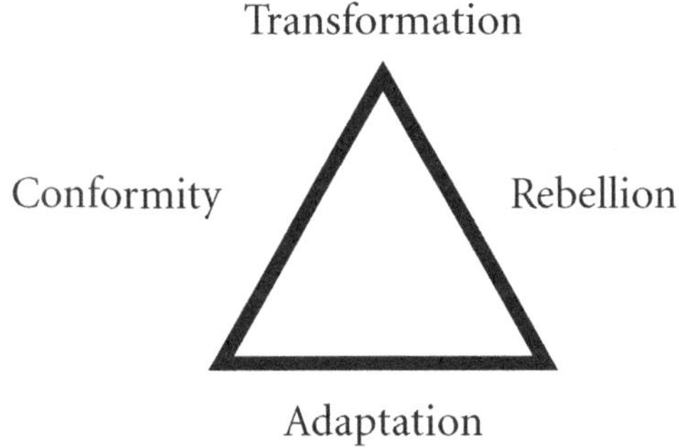
Transformation
Conformity
Rebellion
Adaptation

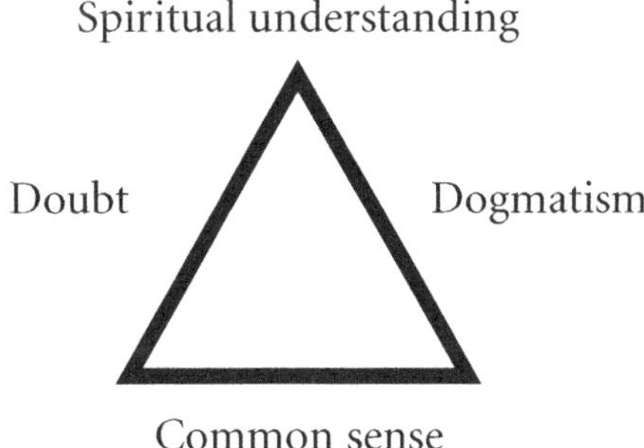
Spiritual understanding
Doubt
Dogmatism
Common sense

Sometimes we become so invested in and identified with an issue that cannot even see the opposite side of it, or the opposite side is so hideous to us that we cannot even allow ourselves to experience it. Some people are obsessively thin; others are morbidly obese. For both groups the compromise is a sensible diet and normal weight. The synthesis is the spiritual understanding that our bodies are temples, we revere them, listen to their wisdom, and eat accordingly.

Some groups in society become so identified with a specific religion that they reject all others as pagan or sinful. They believe no one can know God but a Catholic, or a Baptist, or a Muslim, or a Jew. For some it would be sacrilegious to walk into a temple, mosque, or church. Other groups can't step out of their culture. They want all things American, or English, or German, or Iranian, or Chinese.

Couples start to establish rules and identities right after the wedding. Unconsciously, spouses bring to any union different perceptions of marriage and family from their different families of origin. They may each believe that their family of origin knows better how to live and survive. No matter whom we marry, that person will force us to look at our beliefs about how to live life. Some spouses may even become violent or abusive unless the other agrees with them. When the children come, parents may be even more threatened and alienated from each other.

Family Synthesis is a both-and way of seeing the richness in both spouses' family traditions and allowing both partners and their children their own identities. It is important to realize that most issues lend themselves to compromise and even synthesis. This is possible when a couple keeps always in mind the original love and intent they brought to the marriage, and remember to stay in touch with the good will coming down through the generations into the new family.

EXERCISE: FAMILY SYNTHESIS OF OPPOSITES

Set chairs apart into two teams facing each other. Have another chair set in a triangle from the two opposing teams. You can use a roll of bathroom tissue to draw a line from one set of chairs to the other set, and, in a triangle, to the third chair.

Choose a topic you want to explore and all feel strongly about. If you can't see an opposite view, don't worry. Just experience being strongly invested in this topic. You may even feel stuck and choice-less when it comes to living this topic. For example, you may have to go to work or school, even if you hate it.

Before you start, pick one family member to sit in the third chair. This person will be the observer, the family self, and watch the action of the two sides.

Whatever the issue, seat half the family members in one set of chairs and the others across from them, representing for example:

Doing homework and chores vs. Not doing them

Smiling at people vs. Not smiling

Eating all we want vs. Eating too little

Being friendly vs. Being unfriendly

Having dinners together vs. Not eating together

Taking a vacation vs. Staying home

Buying expensive gadgets vs. Saving money

After choosing the topic, each team needs to talk together and write down all the reasons that their position is correct.

Once everyone is very clear on their position, the teams face each other. Taking turns, each teams tells their position on the topic. It is all right to feel strongly about your position of the topic. The observer should observe, make notes, and be quiet.

Next both teams stand and start moving toward each other. What would a compromise between the two teams look like? Both teams now brainstorm and physically, emotionally, and mentally explore what a possible compromise might be. Remember a compromise incorporates some of both sides of the question.

Still the observer watches and says nothing, but centers on being the family "I" and thinking:

- What is the purpose in what is happening here and how does it reflect this family's Purpose in the world?
- Why do we need two sides to a question?
- What would a synthesis of the two sides look like?
- What potentials and qualities are trying to emerge for this family?
- How does this struggle show or not show the family's inherited identity?

The observer writes down his or her observations.

After the two sides discuss and reach a compromise, the observer tells what he or she has written and can see for the family. Then the whole family stands in the observer's place, looks back on the two sides and the compromise, and experiences the greater meaning of the family. It can see new choices that are more than the compromise. As everyone stands and centers even more on the good will in the family, the family can begin to open to the will of the "I", then to the Will of the Self, finally opening to the Universal Will, which is higher yet.

This exercise can also be done by one person alone. Set up three chairs in a triangle and assign two of them opposite sides of whatever topic you want. Explore fully both sides by sitting in the two opposite chairs, then stand in the middle of them and see the compromise. Then sit in the third chair, become the observer, your "I", knowing it is connected to Purpose, and see what potentials and qualities are trying to happen for you. Align your personal will with the Self and experience a synthesis, something greater than you, a sense of the Universe.

Through the Self-realization that comes when our personal self has a direct awareness of the Self and allows it to direct our lives through the action of our will, we can transcend our limited perspectives. This is usually more personal than familial, but the impact on the family can be great even if other family members resist the direction the Self-realizing individual is taking. Family members need to seek wisdom, faith, and understanding as they support each other in their individual paths of Self-realization.

Psychosynthesis psychologist and analyst Frank Haronian refers to this transcendence and Self-realization as the Sublime. In his article "The Repression of the Sublime," he says individuals and society deny the Sublime and fail to act out of it because they fear the change it might bring to their lives.

When individuals get in touch with the qualities of the Self, they experience freedom as well as responsibility and service. Once we have touched the Sublime, it makes demands on us for expression. If we resist it, we experience anxiety, stress, and depression. Eventually, due to the integrity of Self, we listen and move into action, promoted by the qualities seeking to emerge and express themselves through us.

This is also true for a family. If a family has gotten in touch with its Self, it will seek expression. It may take generations for this expression, or synthesis, to emerge. Until it does, the family may be split into poles, resisting and accepting camps that criticize each other.

RENEE'S STORY

Renee came from a French family. Her father and mother were physicians, divorced, her brother was also a doctor, and her sister was happily married with four children. While in an American college, Renee married an American medical student. To support the two of them during his training, she put aside her own doctoral studies and worked in a job that did not use her talents and intelligence. When he started his private practice, she continued in her job at his insistence and resumed her studies part time.

She resented not being in a position to finish her education full time. She was beginning to want children, but he was not ready to start a family. The marriage was rocky enough when, to make matters worse, she began to suspect that he was having an affair.

Renee's mother and sister traveled from France to support her in her pain. Both told of generations of family women being married to unfaithful husbands, including Renee's father. Her mother said her divorce was the first in a family where women had always stayed with their errant husbands and even had their own affairs.

The following month Renee's father came, with his present girlfriend, and told Renee that he still loved her mother but also wanted his freedom to see other women. Renee realized she was living a generational history for she too was tempted to have an affair in retaliation for her husband's.

While in therapy, she began to question what qualities were getting buried in the history of infidelities. Yes, there was a search for love but also a fear of emotional intimacy with their wives that led the men to go outside their marriages. Renee, breaking with the family pattern, summoned the courage to try to talk to her husband about all her fears and angers. Her effort failed and she sued for divorce. Even before it was final, she wrote, "I have been reminded of my capacity to heal and my light. I am still searching for the true purpose of my existence, but I now know deep in my soul that searching for it is the very motivation of life itself."

The Self always seeks expression through the individual, family, and society by expanding awareness through the "I", or self. If the self can connect more and more with the Self, it can gradually lose its personal identity and become one with the Self.

One person first experienced this in the peace and silence of meditation. He told of imagining sitting with a circle around him with opposites on either side. In the center, he first felt "nothingness" and then "allness"—timelessness, the Universe, and everything in it.

A few days after this experience, he left for a large family reunion. He stated, on returning, that he met family members he had not met or noticed before and that those he had remembered not liking or not liking him had changed and grown. He now found them very interesting and enjoyable. He was able to both participate and choose how he wanted to participate in the reunion in a very individual and positive manner. Because he had touched the Sublime during meditation, he became more aware of his Self and free to make choices and take action in his life.

STAGES OF WILLING

Assagioli notes that while it is wonderful to experience the loving will of the "I" and the Self, ultimately what we learn must be expressed as action. That is why he called his second book *The Act of Will.* It is one thing to intend to do something, even to deliberate doing it. Often it is another thing to follow through with action. This is where many of us get stuck and more miserable than if we had acted.

If we say we hate our job and want to leave it but do nothing to find a new job, our misery grows and we will likely end up fired or laid-off. Just by speaking or thinking our intent, we set change in motion. A woman loved her job but often talked of moving to California to be with family. While she hesitated to make that happen for herself, her job was eliminated and so she was forced to move.

Assagioli identifies six stages of willing and action:

1. Intention—conceiving the purpose
2. Deliberation—considering possibilities
3. Choice—deciding what to do
4. Affirmation—making a statement to be repeated
5. Planning—working out a program of action
6. Execution—acting

EXERCISE: PUTTING FAMILY WILL INTO ACTION

To see how the stages work in family situations, the family chooses a doable goal, something everyone wants, and then acts on that goal. Have paper available to make notes in each step.

1. **INTENTION:** It may take some deliberation to find a goal that meets most of the family's current needs. Start by agreeing to use good will to choose a goal. Clarity and listening to each person's needs is very important. List them. Become quiet and invite the family Self to help with the listening and clarity. What drives and urges have surfaced in the group?

2. **DELIBERATION:** Talk about the possible actions to meet the goal. Allow everyone to see that there are choices, even if some of them seem crazy or wrong. Let everyone's imagination, intuition, thoughts, desires, and body sensations experience the choices. Finally, narrow the choices down to the one that meets the most current need and does the least harm to everyone.

3. **CHOICE:** Decide what actions the family wants to take and not take to meet the goal. Ask how each person will express his or her individuality in this group goal. Keep in mind that people will make mistakes and that the execution will probably need to be fine-tuned several times.

4. **AFFIRMATION:** Let the family make a statement or motto, a powerful phrase that will be a watchword of each individual going through the change. The affirmation can also be an image as well as words, a symbol of what will be accomplished. Make sure the affirmation allows each person to succeed and that it is not a punishment.

5. **PLANNING:** Break the task down into steps. As you review each step, see where you will need strong will, skillful will, and good and loving will. Consider making an outline and a timetable for your plan.

6. **EXECUTION:** Acting on the plan takes constant will, affirmation, and skill. If someone becomes resistant or fails, the family needs skillful, loving, and good will to listen to that person and understand what has gotten in the way. Was the change too hard? Did the outside community fail to reinforce the change? Weekly meetings should be part of the timetable, providing opportunities for family members to affirm and strengthen each other and share the excitement of their achievements. All achievements, no matter how small, build self-esteem in each person and in the family.

EXERCISE: FAMILY WILL QUESTIONNAIRE

This questionnaire is based on one Assagioli wrote in his book on will. It is a summary and reminder of the different aspects of will the family has already explored.

1. **ASPECTS OF WILL:** These include strong, skillful, good and loving, and the Transpersonal Will of the Self. Which are more developed and active in your family and in each member? Which are least developed or under-developed?
2. **QUALITIES OF WILL:** These include energy, intensity, and power; mastery, control, and discipline; concentration, attention, and focus; determination, decisiveness, and promptness; persistence, endurance, and patience; initiative, courage, and daring, and organization, integration, and synthesis. Which are developed and active in your family now? Which are only slightly active? Are they balanced in relationship to each other?
3. **STAGES OF THE WILL:** Remember intention, deliberation, choice, affirmation, planning, and execution. Which stages are more developed for your family? Which need more development?
4. **TRAINING AND DEVELOPMENT OF THE WILL:** What exercises has the family done in recognition of its will? What were the results? What influences have helped in training your family's will? What will project would you like to do next? How can you use will to make changes in the future?

FAMILY FORGIVENESS, GRATITUDE, DREAMS, AND JOY

You have explored your family, as it is today and as it has come down through the generations, to better understand its inherent goodness and capacity for resilience. You have looked at its subpersonalities and how their expectations, desires, and habits determine how you react to any incident. You have also seen that you can disidentify from the generational pain and old habits and re-identify with your family self, accessing your potentials and the strength of the Self and family Purpose. You have learned how your family can use will in all its different aspects to creatively energize itself, making choices, taking action, and promoting goodness and love in the family and the world. But you're not finished yet.

You can move forward by forgiving yourselves and others, developing gratitude to recognize the Holy in your lives, letting your dreams guide you, and opening yourselves to moments of connection that we call joy.

Assagioli once described growth as two steps forward and one back so that we incorporate our past into our present and future. Another time he described growth as an upward, widening spiral that keeps us on one level until we integrate what we have left below. As you looked at your family history, you saw that you could value the past, learn from it, and make choices for the future. The past, the present, and the future all make up your family Purpose.

FORGIVENESS

Forgiveness offers a freedom to any family that uses it. The freedom does not keep us from making mistakes, but by apologizing and asking for forgiveness, we can grow from both our failures and successes. Forgiveness is essential for personal healing and repairing of relationships. It is a voluntary choice or decision, and it requires a shift in our thinking. It takes will to abandon hard feelings toward those we think unjustly injure us, but forgiving them lets us experience compassion, generosity, love, and joy. Knowing this allows us to change and be grateful for the opportunity.

Children learn to say "I'm sorry" and "I forgive you", often without understanding the meaning of the words. Just saying them comes up far short of truly repenting and forgiving, both of which are acts of will—strong, skillful, and good and loving will. Both require understanding that—through humility, trust, choice, and centering on our Self, rather than focusing on our old habits, subpersonalities, and others' perceptions of us—we approach the Presence of God.

Many people believe that to apologize is to admit that they are failures. They forget that we all do wrong. The late theologian Henri Nouwen once said that when we die, we will not look back at our lives and see all the times we failed other people, but rather all the times we did not find ourselves precious and loved by God, all the times we were controlled by the world rather than the Holy.

We all make mistakes, some harmless errors, others hurtful to ourselves and others. We can correct a mistake in our checkbook, but our hurtful words and actions require choosing to apologize and ask forgiveness. The things we don't do—when we fail, for instance to remember others' needs and our own potentials, qualities, and service to others—can also make us suffer. By willfully allowing ourselves to repent, admit our humanity, and let go, we come back into the goodness of our created Purpose. Only when we apologize and accept forgiveness will our suffering end, freeing us to learn and go on with our lives.

When we don't apologize or ask forgiveness, we not only suffer; we grieve. This grieving, often expressing itself as anxiety and depression, results from our failure to stay centered on the truth of who we are and connected to our Self, all our qualities and potentials, and Love.

Those we hurt also suffer and grieve. In their pain, they may assume they have lost a relationship and a future with us, especially since they may not even remember exactly what happened between us. When there is lack of forgiveness with our loved ones and we harbor resentment, they know we are angry. But they may not understand what they have done unless we are willing to tell them.

Often, when we are hurt, our first reaction is to punish the offender and to stay angry in order to protect ourselves and others from more of the same. We refuse to forget, never mind that the offender may have long since, maybe with some regret, moved on. We can do the same, leaving them to their own conscience, freeing ourselves of anger, pain, and any responsibility to change their behavior, when we truly forgive. We may see forgiveness as a risk, but it has great rewards.

Ideally, we would like to be able to talk to the offender about what happened. This is the best way to protect ourselves and prevent repetition of the same behaviors, but sometimes distance and discretion may not allow such a direct approach. Whether you forgive directly or in your heart, the object is, at the very least, to release both parties from preoccupation with the hurtful incident, and, at best, to stop more painful behaviors.

Forgiveness does not require forgetting. Remembering can be helpful, even necessary, so that we can learn what to do in similar situations and build better relationships in the future.

This is especially important when parents divorce yet need to stay in relationship because they have children. Forgiving even an unfaithful, abusive, or addicted ex-spouse releases the forgiver from pain and codependency and gives the forgiven sole responsibility for his or her anger, guilt, actions, and emotional work.

Families also can wound, suffer, and grieve each other by forgetting their purpose and failing to forgive. To change or prevent this behavior, parents can start by apologizing for their own misbehaviors to the children and each other, communicating their hurts, and saying, "I forgive you" for all to hear. Observing this, children can learn to ask for and accept forgiveness from one another.

EXERCISE: FORGIVENESS ONE-ON-ONE

This exercise is for two family members—parents, children, or one of each—when one of them has offended the other.

Stand or sit the two people facing each other, quietly centering and choosing to listen to each other with their skillful, good and loving will. First the offended person describes the mental, physical, and emotional impact of the hurt.

Then the offender says, "I hear you say that I___________. I am sorry and I hope you will forgive me." It is important that the offender owns the hurtful behavior and does not try to give a long defensive explanation of it. Keep it simple.

The hurt person responds: "I forgive you and I forgive me for my part in what happened." The two stand together, picturing a beam of light coming down on them and into their hearts to heal the pain. They remember the love that exists in their family.

EXERCISE: FAMILY FORGIVENESS

This exercise is designed for the family when it has been offended or criticized by one or more extended family members, neighbors, schoolmates, co-workers, or others. As with individuals, the offenders may not have apologized and may even continue the same hurtful behaviors unless the family is able talk to them about the situation.

Set up two chairs facing each other, or designate two facing places in a room. The whole family sits or stands behind one chair or in one place that represents the injured family members.

LEADER:

"Using your skillful will, imagine the person or people who caused the pain sitting or standing across from you. Visualize how they look, talk, and act toward you and others. You can almost smell them as they become real to you.

"Now each of you tell them just how you feel and think about yourself, your involvement, and what you see has happened in the incident. Tell of your hurt from your heart. Support each other in the pain and tell what each of you sees or remembers of the incident. *[Pause for discussion]*

"Now leave the seats or space you are in and go to the space of the person or persons who have offended the family.

"Again, using your imagination and intuition, become the perpetrator or one of that group. How do you feel about yourself? How do you think about yourself? What is your body like? Make this person more and more real to you. Take turns telling each other what it feels like to be this person.

"Now look across at the other chair or space that belongs to the family and tell it why you are angry and defensive and what your motivation was for saying or doing what you did to them. Fully tell them how you feel.

"Family, go back to your original family place. Sit down and take in what the other person or people have said. It doesn't matter whether they are right or wrong. You may absolutely disagree, but at least you heard them. What insights have you gained about what happened? *[Pause for discussion]*

"Now quiet down, slowly center, and allow yourself to see a beam of light from the family Self come down into the room, onto each person's head, and into each person's heart. As each person centers on the light in their heart, see the person or people you need to forgive in front of you and say out loud the following affirmation:

"'I freely and fully forgive you and release you and set you free. I accept your forgiveness of me. I send you my blessing and my love and know we are each free for healing love to live in us.'

"As you say these words, experience the release, peace, love, and freedom."

If the hurt has been deep and long-lasting, print the affirmation on cards for family members to carry with them. Each should repeat this affirmation ten times a day for six weeks, and slowly the release will occur.

GRATITUDE

Assagioli states that gratitude is the highest aspect and manifestation of love. Gratitude, like forgiveness, is an act of will, a recognition of the possibilities in the Self and the limits of our humanity. To be grateful, we have to step past our angers, disappointments, and expectations in our subpersonalities, go into our "I", and allow connection with the Self. Research has found that our depression lifts if they learn to continuously thank their Self, a Higher Power, or the Universe for the smallest details of their lives. For example, first thing in the morning, say "thank you" for awakening. As you put your feet on the floor, thank the Powers of the world for your ability to put your feet out of bed. As you use the toilet, thank God and your body and its most basic functions. As you brush your teeth, taste the toothpaste and experience your ability to brush, and thank the Universe for this simple task. As you dress, be thankful for clothes to choose and your ability to button and zip. Continue through breakfast preparation and eating. Meet every part of the day at school, work, or home with gratitude that you can act, respond, and participate in the world in your own way.

As we appreciate the very simplest physical tasks and our ability to perform them, we begin to sense a deeper gratitude for each day and for life itself. Gratitude becomes a mantra or prayer we say continuously all day, recognizing the simplest of miracles and goodness. To start your prayer or meditation time with a mantra of "thank you" allows a centering and deepening even when your life is in turmoil. A Buddhist disciple describes gratitude as the recognition of the Grace of God and the realization that "we are like sails, catching the wind of God." When goodness seems to elude us in times of crisis, we can still find the smallest things to feel grateful for and transform the darkest hours into moments of learning and love.

Gratitude acknowledges the gifts the Universe is constantly showering down on us. As we are grateful to ourselves and others, we see the thoughtfulness and love in all of these gifts and become aware that we have value to others and to creation, a sense of Purpose in life.

As a family opens up to the gifts of each member and the inherited gifts from past generations, it experiences a greater sense of Purpose. When spouses are grateful for each other, they may realize that they were right in marrying each other and that their choice of spouse has Purpose and meaning, even if the marriage has problems with abuse, addiction, suicide, illness, divorce, and other dysfunctions. Instead of blaming themselves for making the wrong choice, they may become more aware of their capacities to live as fully as possible as individuals while supporting each other's growth. Gratitude between marriage partners reinforces new ways of behaving, not just with each other but also with other family members.

When each family member can be grateful and remember to thank other members of the family, each will feel valued and supported, and the family will be stronger and more resilient in times of challenge.

EXERCISE: FAMILY GRATITUDE

Ask each family member to find little ways to anonymously give to or acknowledge other family members during the week. The gifts may be tangible or, better yet, favors done for one another, small acts of caring. At the end of the week, in a family meeting ask each person to acknowledge the gifts they have given. Those who have received gifts should say "thank you" for each caring gift. The family may then set aside a certain night during the week for the recognition of gifts.

Brent Atkinson, a psychologist and couples therapist, recommends that couples keep week-long journals, noting those "extra-positive moments" when the other partner says a kind word or makes a non-verbal gesture of affection, times when they feel extra-positive about a family member and their relationship, and at least one good time they shared. At the end of the week, in a family meeting, the couple shares their experiences.

To start or end any meeting, have each person in the family say one word that tells what they are grateful for in the family. Then take turns facing a family member and saying,

"I am happy that we have__________________ in the family
Family Member Name

because____."

This technique can be also used in gatherings that include extended family and close friends, such as a Thanksgiving holiday dinner. Give everyone a slip of paper with some other guest's name on it, and when all are seated, go around the table, asking each to read the name on their slip of paper and say,

"I am happy we have__________________ here today
Family Member Name

because____."

For another exercise in family gratitude, go back to the animal exercise in Chapter 2. Ask each person, as their animal, what he or she has since learned about the family, what new skills they have learned living in it, what they would say today about it, and how they would show gratitude for being in it. Have everyone draw a picture, write a story, or develop an image that describes their progress and gratitude.

DREAMS

Dreams, with their magical, mysterious, and often prophetic qualities, have fascinated mankind from the beginning. Not only shamans, witch doctors, priests, kings, and emperors but all of us have experienced the power of dreams and acted on them, for good or evil.

Early in the twentieth century, Freud found dreams so important to his study of the unconscious that he wrote on the interpretation of them. His most prominent students—Assagioli, Jung, and Adler—also understood the importance of dreams and incorporated them in their psychologies. Sociologists and anthropologists discovered and are still studying the use of dreams in Native American cultures. Anthropologist Kilton Stewart studied the Senoi people of Malaya, known as the "dream people," and how they used dreams to guide them in their social, cultural, and personal lives toward harmony, peace, and well-being.

Every morning men, women, and children gathered and told of their dreams of the night before. They believed the dreams were real and so planned activities, learned songs, composed poems, designed dances, and found places to hunt, all from their dreams. Most important to them was to finish dreams, so they encouraged each other to re-dream their dreams, believing that they could gain some new understanding and spiritual insight. Other times, having agreed to try to dream on some community issue, they used their morning meetings to share their communal dreams for insight on how to move forward.

There are many books on dreams, their symbols, and interpretations. Unfortunately, interpretation gets between the dreamer and the dream by tying it to the interpreter's perspective. The understanding and meaning of a dream is in the dreamer.

Jung said that to understand the meaning of a dream, the dreamer needs to "actualize" it by willingly remembering all the action in it and reliving it with an analyst or a group. Psychosynthesists do similarly while also encouraging dreamers to know they have choices and will and, if necessary, a wise figure of their choice to walk with them through the dream.

Some people have trouble remembering their dreams, so it is helpful to have pen and paper at your bedside to immediately write your dreams down whenever you wake up. People who have recurrent dreams and nightmares especially need to do this in order to bring them to resolution. With will and practice, we can learn how to dream purposefully about subjects of our choice and to repeat old dreams but with different endings. From this discipline, we can recognize symbols and patterns in our dreams and use them purposefully to listen to our unconscious for insight into how to deal with our problems and get on with our lives. When actualizing dreams, dreamers need to know whether they are active participants or observers in the dreams. Sometimes dreamers can even say, "I am dreaming now," analyze the dream, gain insight, try different endings, and be aware that they are manipulating the dream.

Dreams can originate from the Self, which presents them to communicate with our consciousness. These dreams are the Self working to point out to us how we will be or have been living our lives. Through dreams, the Self questions and challenges our awareness, attitudes, and choices and presents other options more in tune with our potentials and Purpose.

EXERCISE: FAMILY DREAMS

Families can use dreams to discover the direction they are moving, heal problems, confront fears, and encourage faith in their unconscious, or family Self.

At first, simply sharing dreams with each other at a family meeting with everyone listening from a centered, non-judgmental place will build closeness in the family. Sharing our unconscious process makes us vulnerable, but having it accepted builds trust. Like sharing, listening is also an act of will, requiring intuition, thoughtfulness, imagination, sensation, feeling, and impulses. There may be a great temptation to interpret someone else's dream. However, it is important, when adding your thoughts and intuitions, to speak carefully from your experience so that the dream stays with the dreamer. Dream analyst Jeremy Taylor suggests that the feedback begin with the phrase, "If this were my dream ____________." Then the dreamer can choose whether to use the added material. If dreamers have trouble working with their dream, Taylor asks them to stop, look around, and tell what they see and hear.

Like the Senoi, families can do collective dreamwork and use it to better understand and strengthen themselves and explore choices. They can also use dreamwork in times of crisis to gain resilience and grow.

Some questions family members might ask about a dream are:

- What is the dream saying?
- What is it asking of us?
- What are the major symbols, issues, conflicts, and unresolved situations in the dream?
- What are the various feelings and actions in the dream?
- Is there an adversary or someone wounded in the dream?
- Is there a healing or helping force in the dream?
- Why did this dream happen in our family?

- Why is it important to the family?
- What does the experience in the dream teach us?
- How can we change as a result of this experience?
- What is the essence, or chief value, we gained from this dream?
- What would happen to us if we willfully listened to this dream and acted on it?

Question 19 in the Family Synthesis Questionnaire was about dreams through your family's generations and how they might have changed your family for the better or worse. Look back at your answers and reflect on whether the family has fulfilled those dreams. Can you disidentify from those old dreams enough to see a purpose in them? Is that purpose relevant today?

Now is a good time to ask if the family wants to go to sleep with the old family dream and Purpose in mind and see what new dreams come. If anyone or all set this goal, be sure you have a family meeting to discuss what you have all dreamed.

The family can also do dreamwork about a current family issue. After phrasing the issue as clearly as possible, agree one night to ask for guidance and dreams about it. Be sure everyone journals their dreams. The next day listen to each other's dreams. They may vary greatly, but each will have some thread of wisdom. It may take days or weeks before all the alternatives for dealing with the issue come out. Meanwhile, everyone in the family will feel they contributed and that there is truly a family Self guiding the family.

JOY

As we are connected with our unconscious through our dreams, as we learn to have the freedom forgiveness offers, and feel gratitude, we often experience something we call happiness and even joy. Joy comes of being open to unconditional love and connection with your Self, and it results in an expansion of consciousness and an experience of inclusiveness and of all of life's best qualities.

Bonnano says one of the attributes of resilient people is positive emotion. Seligman, founder of Positive Psychology, focuses on people's strengths, talents, and virtues rather than their pathology. He sees happiness as derived from the courage to cope, which builds self-esteem. Positive Psychology is a psychology of possibility, asking people to become more than they imagined they could be. Positive psychologists investigate compassion, service, forgiveness, love, and their relationship to health. They want to find out what supports a sense of well-being rather than just disease. They stress spiritual practices such as meditation and how it enhances people and contributes to their health.

Psychiatrist and genetics professor C. Robert Cloninger says happiness consists of kindness, an attitude of accomplishment, an ability to solve problems, and an awareness of something universal beyond the individual self. He adds that people who have these attributes are rarely angry and have friends, a resilient sense of well-being, and many positive emotions and experiences. Having wealth, fame, or power is not important to them.

Cloninger says that about fifty percent of our capacity for happiness is inherited and that we can become happier by learning to strengthen character traits such as tolerance, compassion, responsibility, resourcefulness, spirituality, intuition, and service to others. He believes intuition connects us with each other and nature and that spirituality has at its core joy, or connection with the infinite. In other words, while a "talent" for happiness is gene-determined, we can pursue it by thwarting negative emotions such as pessimism, resentment, and anger and fostering the positive emotions of empathy, serenity, and gratitude.

Happiness, then, is an achievement, an intention, or act of will, a mindful choice of positive attitudes and behaviors that open us to new experiences, passions, and connections and allow us to let go of old perceptions and fears.

Psychiatrist George Vaillant says that humans are wired not only for survival like other animals but also for positive emotions and spirituality, and the most dramatic spiritual experience is joy. Joy is the least studied emotion, the one we most search for, and a connection with a power greater than ourselves. He says, "Happiness displaces pain, and joy embraces it." Joy can be with us in times of great happiness and great grief.

To Assagioli joy is "the song of the soul" with "clear high notes" that "bring peace… to others." It is "vivifying," "healing," "flaming," and "radiant." "Joy makes you invulnerable," he writes. "Teach the joy of beauty, teach the happiness of wisdom, and teach the bliss of love."

Wisdom is foresight, empathy, discernment, and good judgment. It is the ability to see clearly our inspirations and intuitions, our path to our greatest good, and the possibility of achieving our purpose. Assagioli describes it as the "harmonious interweaving of the individual plan with the Universal Plan, and the will to retain firm control of the rudder and proceed on a straight course."

Wisdom allows us to recognize life's follies and our own seriousness so that we can laugh at ourselves and with others. When we do this, we often feel the joy that accompanies moments of inspiration when we touch the Divine.

As a family, be connected to each other with laughter and joy. Enjoy each other and all you can be.

EXERCISES: PERSONAL JOY

Joy can be remembered and cultivated. For all the exercises below, center first, close your eyes, and calm. Torkom Saraydarian, a spiritual guru, designed the following exercises and recommended doing one of them at least three times a week. Do them patiently and not before bedtime or you will be too energized to sleep.

1. Remember the earliest joy you experienced. See how old you were, where you were, and who, if anyone, was with you—all the details of that first experience. Fully re-experience that joyous time in your body, then your feelings, then your thoughts. You are now experiencing joy in the present, as you did in the past.
2. Remember when you witnessed someone else feeling real joy. Observe how it affected that person physically, emotionally, and mentally. Now share the memory of their joy in yourself in the present.
3. Remember and re-experience a time when you gave someone else joy.
4. Remember and re-experience a time when someone intentionally gave you joy.
5. Remember the joys of nature—flowers, meadows, rivers, sea, waterfalls, animals, sunlight, soft breezes, mountains, sand, and so on.
6. Radiate joy throughout your body, emotions, and mind. Really sense joy in your body, in your face, on your tongue, in your head, down your arms, through all your organs, down your legs, into your feet and connected with the Earth. Let the energy of the earth come back up through your legs, into your body, your spine, and your head and connect with the light above your head. Let your emotions tune into this energy traveling back and forth from ground to above. As this energy of connection moves through you, let your thoughts also connect and radiate joy. Become one with Earth and sun and Universe. Experience joy.

7. Imagine a future event, see yourself there with others, and radiate joy into it. See the success of that future event, enterprise, or special work you will be doing. Visualize your highest dream actualized and infused with joy.
8. Create a new identity by making a list of thirty or so good qualities you have stored in you. Express one quality today, a different one tomorrow, and so on, but do not expect others to recognize them in you. This is for you. As you act out each one on your list, do you find more?
9. Meditate on joy. Relax physically, emotionally, and mentally. Inhale joy into your being, and exhale joy three times. See above your head a beautiful rainbow. Let the beauty of the rainbow fill you. Become each color and feel the joy in its special gift. Let all the colors fill you. Think, "Joy is harmony between the Self and the Universal Self. It is infinite."

EXERCISE: FAMILY JOY

Sit together in a circle or a line, close enough to be able to hold each others' hands.

LEADER:

"Center on all the love, gratitude, laughter, and positive emotion you can remember feeling when we are together. Holding hands, close your eyes, and picture you and your family once again on a path, walking together. Be aware of each other and the support you can give each other. Notice that the path is wide enough so that you can all walk comfortably hand in hand. The warm sun overhead reminds you that always with you are your family "I" and family Self. Quietly experience their wisdom for your family. Now look around you and see the colors and scenery as you all walk together.

"Begin to be aware that behind you and to the side, others are also walking. They are your grandparents, aunts, uncles, and cousins. Take time to note them and feel the blood relationship that you have with each other. Become aware of all the generations of ancestors also walking behind you, encouraging your family to move forward, grow, and be courageous as you walk into the unknown future.

"Again, become aware of the sun overhead, shining down on the family and the family "I". Using your imagination, will, and intuition, fully allow the family "I" to be there with your family, and experience its connection with the light of the family Self and its ability to guide you on the path.

"Look ahead and see that the path has smaller paths coming off it on either side. As a family, choose one of those side paths and see where it goes. See also what you would experience if you did not take your awareness of your family Self with you but chose to be separate and walk without your guide. Talk with each other about the experience of a side path with no light and no Self. *[Pause for discussion.]*

"As a family, come back to the main path and feel united with all the generations and your Purpose and Self. You can still see the other paths and realize that there are many roads and choices your family has made in the past and will make in the future. Some of these will separate you from your Purpose, and others will only diversify and increase your sense of Purpose and Self.

"Again, be aware of each other. Breathe deeply and experience the connection you have with each other, all the generations, and now with even more, with humanity. Feel a sense of human purpose, of a connection and joining together to a greater Universal Purpose, a Universal Path. Be connected to the Universe, the Creator, all you are, can be, and will be. See the light leading everyone forward to a greater awareness and connection. Feel the joy and affirmation of purpose for each of you and for your family all together. See each of you walking forward individually on your path, joined with your family, and with all mankind connected to the light and joy. Experience JOY."

You and your family have come a long way toward finding your Purpose and your relationship with your potential. You have embarked on a journey of not only lifetime but of many lifetimes. Thank your ancestors for struggling, and congratulate yourselves for beginning your journey and stepping forward into your future.

QUALITIES

Acceptance
Admiration
Appreciation
Awe

Beauty
Being
Bliss
Brotherhood

Calm
Caring
Communication
Compassion
Comprehension
Conviction
Cooperation
Courage
Creativity

Decisiveness
Delight
Discernment
Discipline

Ecstasy
Elegance
Energy
Enthusiasm
Eternity

Faith
Forgiveness
Freedom
Friendship

Generosity
Goodness
Goodwill
Grace
Gratitude

Harmony
Humor

Inclusiveness
Infinity

Joy

Liberation
Light
Love
Loyalty

Non-attachment

Order

Patience
Peace
Persistence
Power
Purpose

Quiet

Reality
Receptivity
Renewal
Responsiblity
Risk

Serenity
Service
Silence
Simplicity
Sisterhood
Strength
Synthesis

Trust
Truth

Understanding
Unity
Universality

Vitality

Wholeness
Will (strong, skillful, good, and loving)
Wisdom
Wonder

Please add more of your own.

QUALITIES OF WILL

Energy, Dynamic Power, Intensity

Mastery, Control, Discipline

Concentration, Attention, One-Pointedness, Focus

Determination, Decisiveness, Resoluteness, Promptness

Persistence, Endurance, Patience

Initiative, Courage, Daring

Organization, Integration, Synthesis

Please add more of your own.

FOR THERAPISTS

This book was written for families to use for their own growth, but it could easily be used by other groups and therapists dedicated to growth and spiritual exploration. It is assumed that any group leader or therapist fully reads the book first and experiences the theory and exercises for themselves.

Psychosynthesis therapists must first know themselves based on knowledge of their own subpersonalities, or defense mechanisms, their emerging potentials, and their experience of Self, which they gain through their own training and therapy. As Assagioli states, "Before being able to communicate Psychosynthesis to others, we must have experienced it in depth in ourselves. Intellectual knowledge is not sufficient to grasp the spirit of Psychosynthesis. Each technique must be tried out at length on oneself." Training in Psychosynthesis has no end for it is an open system with only some "temporary halting places."

For Assagioli, the goals of Psychosynthesis therapy are:

1. ***Thorough knowledge of one's personality:*** Using tests, genograms, questionnaires, timelines, and exercises to uncover the subpersonalities and their images that obsess and secretly dominate us and all areas of the unconscious, including our latent talents and spiritual potentials.
2. ***Control of the Various Elements of the Personality:*** Using our will and the disidentification exercise to make us mindful of our harmful images and behaviors, so that we can learn to make choices that free us and allow us to reach our potential.
3. ***Realization of One's True Self—The Discovery or Creation of a Unifying Center:*** Using ideal models and other techniques to discover and know our own inner experience of Self rather than other people's view of us.
4. ***Psychosynthesis: the Formation or Reconstruction of the Personality Around the New Center:*** Developing latent aspects of the personality, thereby creating a firm organization of the personality through which the Self can be expressed.

Like Psychosynthesis therapy, Family Synthesis therapy starts with a review of the unique situation and problems of each client. Through inventories, questionnaires, timelines, and awareness exercises, this book can help therapists explore a family's personality. While all listen to the family story, the therapist begins treatment by both working with the painful emotions, thoughts, and behaviors, and also using active techniques to uncover the potentials and qualities struggling for expression.

Before each family session, the therapist scans his or her own body, emotions, and mind, and centers, going to the place of the "I" and Self. When meeting the clients and starting the session, the therapist senses the light over his or her own head and the head of each client in the room. In this way the therapist allows the Self to direct the session and sees not only the clients' discomfort and pain, but also the qualities trying to emerge in their lives. It is in this connection with the different Selves in the room that the therapy takes place, with the therapist assuming an underlying health even in the presence of disease.

While taking the time for everyone to hear the family narrative as thoroughly and clearly as possible, the therapist models the structure of the family meeting by pointing out the importance of maintaining a non-judgmental attitude, being open to all answers, holding material private in the family, and journaling.

When it seems appropriate to the family process, the therapist can introduce "Who Am I", "Walking the Egg Diagram," "The Evening Review," the disidentification exercise, or a purpose exercise so that the family can start to experience its "I". If the family acknowledges a wall between itself and others, the therapist can do the "Will and the Wall of Fear" exercise.

Will, a concept unique to Psychosynthesis and Family Synthesis, can be introduced at any time the family is ready to train its energy toward changing behaviors, making choices, and taking action toward goals, growth and self-actualization.

The earlier will exercises, such as "Using Strong Will to Change Behavior," "The Family Star Diagram," "Role Playing Habits," and the "Family Will

Questionnaire" can be done, with some explanation, during earlier phases of counseling. After the concepts of will and choice have been introduced, any of the other will exercises can follow. These include "The Ideal Model," which is very important for establishing the concept of the Family Self.

Exercises on forgiveness and gratitude can also be done at any time. Family dreams be started fairly early as a way to reveal the power of the unconscious. Joy can occur at any moment in the awareness process and should be acknowledged, greeted as a connection with the spiritual, and celebrated by all.

For all therapists wishing training:

- The Association for the Advancement of Psychosynthesis lists North American sites at www.aap-psychosynthesis.org.
- For sites in Australia, Austria, Brazil, Canada, Denmark, France, Germany, Greece, Ireland, Israel, Italy, Mexico, Netherlands, New Zealand, Norway, Poland, Portugal, Russia, Spain, Sweden, Switzerland, and the United Kingdom, see http://two.not2.org/psychosynthesis/centers.

GENOGRAMS

A genogram is a type of family tree that describes the family structure, interactions, medical history, education, occupations, religious affiliations and changes, and any other important generational information.

The material used in this appendix is taken from the following internet sites:

www.genopro.com • www.genogramanalytics.com • www.wikipedia.com
http://faculty-web.at.northwestern.edu/commstud/galvin/More%20Genograms/

Each image is reproduced as "fair use" from respective sites. My original source was McGoldrick, Gerson, and Shellenberger's book, *Genograms: Assessment and Intervention.* Their book tells how to build a genogram and gives and interprets the genograms of many famous families. It is well worth having in a library.

The genogram or tree is created using squares as males and circles as females. A line going between a square and a circle denotes marriage. The children of the marriage are shown by vertical lines down from the horizontal marriage line. The person that is the primary perspective of the genogram has double lines—either a double square or a double circle to identify them. Each preceding generation follows the same symbols.

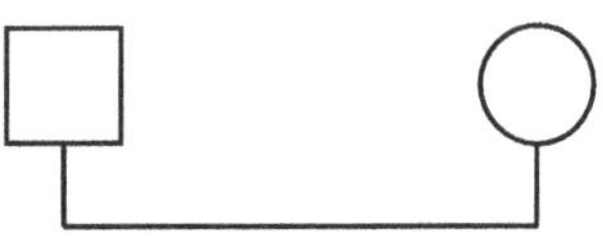

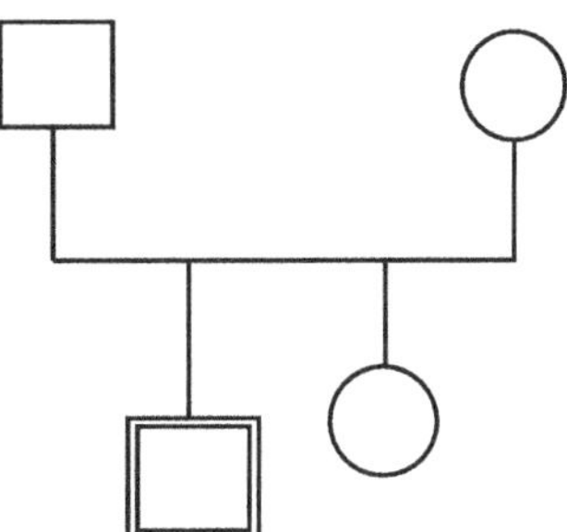

The standard symbols for a genogram used by www.genogramanalytic.com and McGoldrick are:

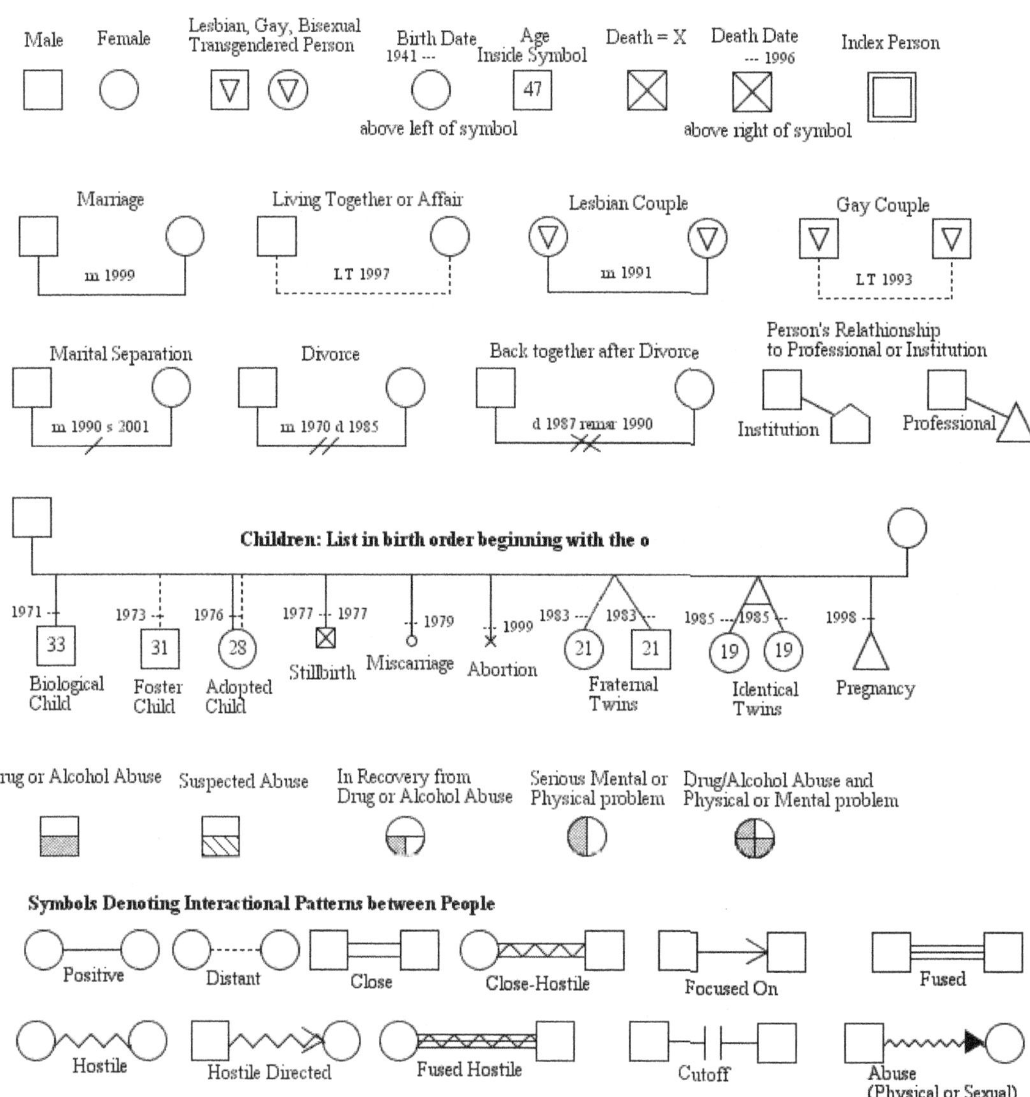

Sample Genogram created by GenoPro

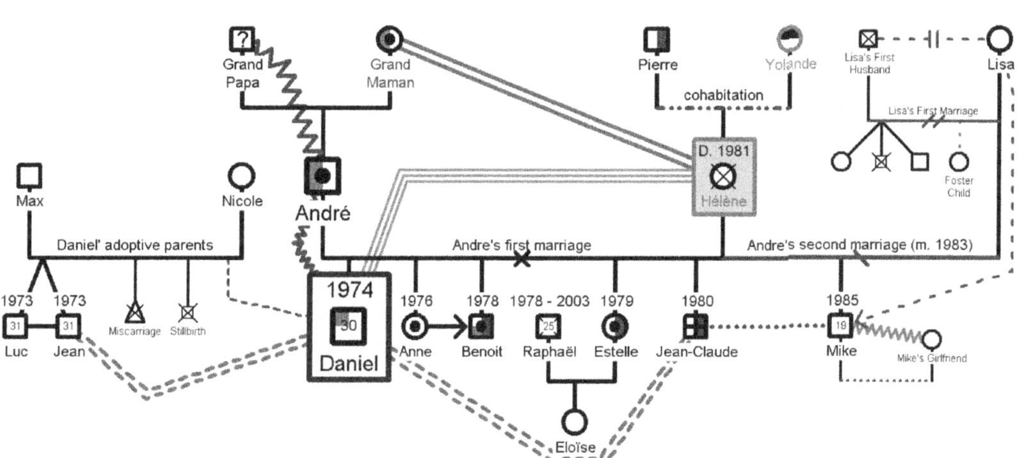

Besides names, birth and death dates, the genogram should also include occupations, diseases and causes of deaths, wars, world or family catastrophes, geographic moves, ethnic background and migration dates for the families of both parents and everyone living in the current household. If at all possible, note relationships with the lines showing both the loving and the conflicted ones. If you can remember a family motto or purpose, put that down or put it at the bottom of your genogram with the name of who said or lived this purpose.

If you were adopted or fostered and don't know your family of origin, use the family you know. You were still influenced by them and their relationships and stories. If there is some material you don't know, ask extended family such as cousins, aunts, grandparents, old family friends, and even old neighbors. Everyone likes to tell stories and help fill in background information.

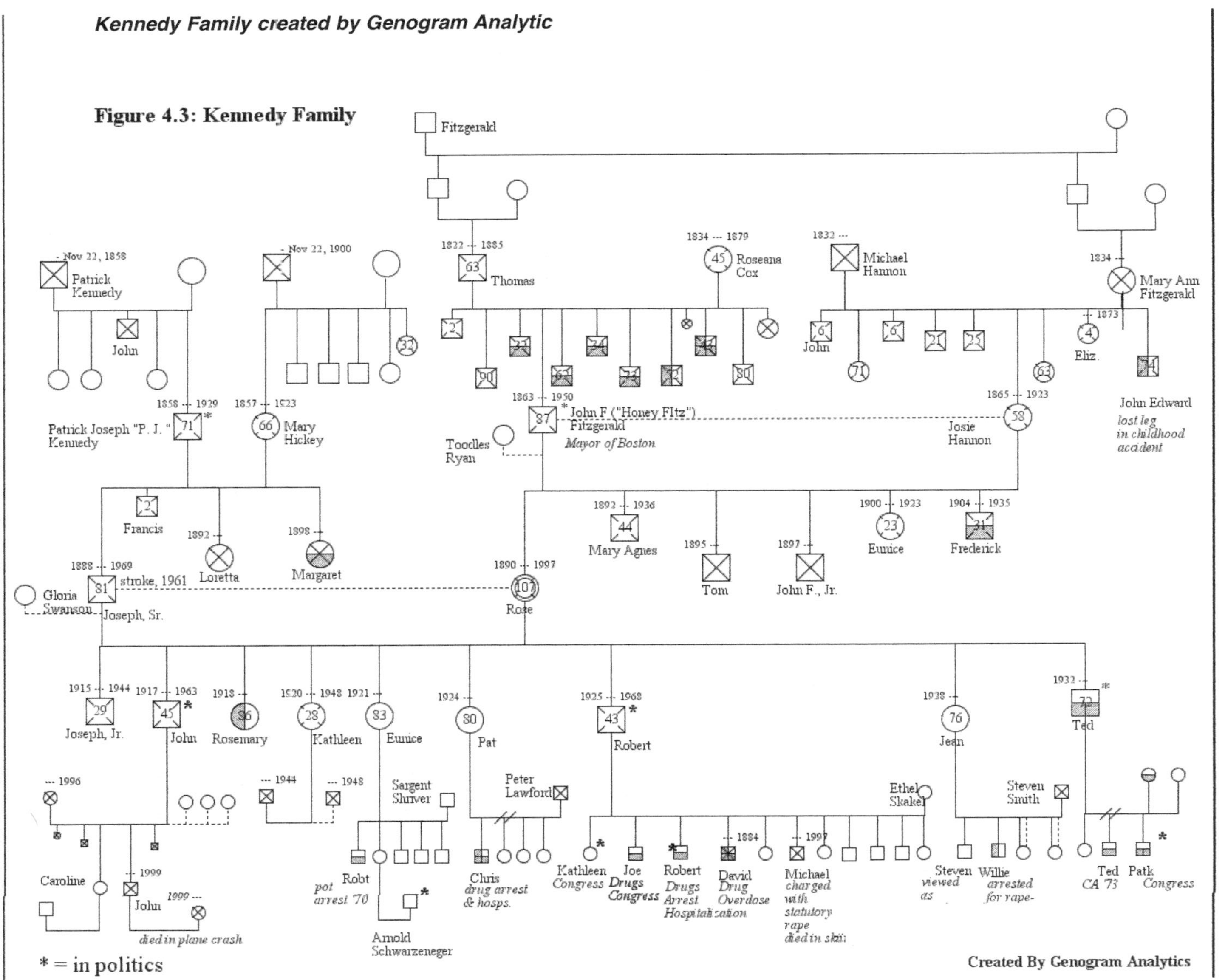

Kennedy Family created by Genogram Analytic
Figure 4.3: Kennedy Family
Fitzgerald
1822 -- 1885
Thomas
1834 --- 1879
Roseana Cox
1832 ---
Michael Hannon
1834
Mary Ann Fitzgerald
1873
Eliz.
John Edward
lost leg in childhood accident
Nov 22, 1858
Patrick Kennedy
John
Nov 22, 1900
John
1858 -- 1929
Patrick Joseph "P. J." Kennedy
1857 -- 1923
Mary Hickey
1863 -- 1950
John F ("Honey Fitz") Fitzgerald
Mayor of Boston
Toodles Ryan
1865 -- 1923
Josie Hannon
Francis
1892
Loretta
1898
Margaret
1888 -- 1969
stroke, 1961
Gloria Swanson
Joseph, Sr.
1890 -- 1997
Rose
1892 -- 1936
Mary Agnes
1895
Tom
1897
John F., Jr.
1900 -- 1923
Eunice
1904 -- 1935
Frederick
1915 -- 1944
Joseph, Jr.
1917 -- 1963
John
1918
Rosemary
1920 -- 1948
Kathleen
1921
Eunice
1924
Pat
1925 -- 1968
Robert
1928
Jean
1932
Ted
--- 1996
Caroline
1999
John
1999 ---
died in plane crash
--- 1944
--- 1948
Sargent Shriver
Robt
pot arrest '70
Arnold Schwarzeneger
Peter Lawford
Chris
drug arrest & hosps.
Ethel Skakel
Kathleen
Congress
Joe
Drugs
Congress
Robert
Drugs
Arrest
Hospitalization
1884
David
Drug
Overdose
1997
Michael
charged with statutory rape
died in skii
Steven
viewed as
Steven Smith
Willie
arrested for rape-
Ted
CA 73
Patk
Congress
* = in politics
Created By Genogram Analytics

You can use this page to draw your own genogram or use a bigger sheet of paper. Whatever you use, save it in your family box.

Alcott, L. M. (2004). *Little Women.* New York: Sterling.

American Psychological Association (2002). Ten ways to build resilience, *The road to resilience.* Brochure distributed as part of a tool kit published by the Discovery Health Channel and APA. Washington, D.C.

Anderson, J. M. (1989). *Basics of group psychosynthesis.* 7370 N. Meadowdale Rd., Edmonds, WA.

Assagioli, R. (1959). *Dynamic psychology and psychosynthesis.* New York: Psychosynthesis Research Foundation.

Assagioli, R. (1965). *Psychosynthesis: A manual of principles and techniques.* New York: Viking Press.

Assagioli, R. (1965). *Psychosynthesis: Individual and social.* New York: Psychosynthesis Research Foundation.

Assagioli, R. (1966). *The training of the will.* New York: Psychosynthesis Research Foundation.

Assagioli, R. (1967). *Jung and psychosynthesis.* New York: Psychosynthesis Research Foundation.

Assagioli, R. (1972). *The balancing and synthesis of opposites.* New York: Psychosynthesis Research Foundation.

Assagioli, R. (1974). *The act of will.* New York: Penguin.

Assagioli, R. (1991). *Transpersonal development.* London: Crucible/Harper Collins.

Athanasius, Bishop of Alexandria [373], from Wright, J. (1991), *Readings for the Daily Office from the early church.* New York: Church Publishing.

Atkinson, B. (2007). *Emotional intelligence in couples therapy: Advances in neurobiology and the science of intimate relationships.* Workshop presented in St. Louis by Atkinson of The Couples Research Institute in Geneva, IL.

Baldwin, J. (1995). *The fire next time.* New York: Modern Library.

Bandler, R. and Grinder, J. (1975). *The structure of magic,* Vols. I and II. Palo Alto, CA: Science and Behavior Books.

Beavers, W. R. (1986). *Successful marriages.* New York: W.W. Norton.

Beck, A. (1982). Achieving freedom through forgiveness. *Journal of Religion and Applied Behavioral Sciences,* vol. III, (3), *25-28.* Syracuse, NY: Association for Creative Change.

Beavers, W. R. and Hampson, R. B. (1990). *Successful Families: Assessment and intervention.* New York: W.W. Norton.

Becvar, D. S. and Becvar, R. J. (1988). *Family therapy: A systematic integration.* Boston, Allyn & Bacon.

Becvar, D. S. (2007). *Families that flourish.* New York, W.W. Norton.

Bernard, J. (1982). *The future of marriage.* New Haven, CT: Yale University Press.

Bettleheim, B. (1984). *Freud and man's soul.* New York: Vintage Books, Random House.

Bonanno, G. (2004). Loss, Trauma, and Human Resilience. *American Psychologist*, 59, (1). American Psychological Association: Washington, D.C.

Bronfenbrenner, U. (1979). *The ecology of human development.* Cambridge, MA: Harvard University Press.

Boszormenyi-Nagy, I. and Spark, G. (1973). *Invisible loyalties: Reciprocity in intergenerational family therapy.* New York: Harper & Row.

Bowen, M. (1976). Theory in the practice of psychotherapy, and Principles and techniques of multiple family therapy. P. J. Guerin (Ed.), *Family therapy: Theory and practice.* New York: Gardner Press.

Bowen, M. (1978). *Family therapy in clinical practice.* New York: Aronson.

Brazelton, T. B. (1981). *On becoming a family: The growth of attachment.* New York: Delacorte.

Brown, M. Y. (1993). *Growing whole: Self-realization on an endangered planet.* Mt. Shasta, CA: Psychosynthesis Press.

Brown, M. Y. (2004). *The unfolding self.* New York: Helios Press.

Burns, D. (1999). *Feeling good.* New York: HarperCollins.

Campbell, S. (1988). *The couple's journey: Intimacy as a path to wholeness.* San Luis Obispo, CA: Impact Publishers.

Capacchione, L. (1979). *The creative journal: The art of finding yourself.* Athens, Ohio: Ohio University Press.

Carter, B. and McGoldrick, M. (Eds.). (1998). *The expanded life cycle: Individual, family, and community.* Needham Heights, MA: Allyn and Bacon.

Cloninger, C. R. (2004). *Feeling good: the science of well-being.* New York: Oxford University Press.

Conger, R. D. & Conger, K. J. (2002). Resilience in Midwestern families: Selected findings from the first decade of a prospective, longitudinal study. *Journal of Marriage and Family,* 64, 361-373.

Coontz, S. (1997). *The way we really are: Coming to terms with America's changing families.* New York: Basic Books.

Cooperman, J. B. (2007). The pursuit of happiness. *St. Louis magazine,* vol. 13, 3.

Crampton, M. (1968). *The visual "Who Am I?" method: An approach to experience of the Self.* New York: Psychosynthesis Research Foundation Issue No. 23.

Crampton, M. (1969). *The use of mental imagery in psychosynthesis.* New York: Psychosynthesis Research Foundation.

Crampton, M. (1972). *Toward a psychosynthetic approach to the group.* New York: Psychosynthesis Research Foundation.

Crampton, M. (1974). *Psychological Energy transformations: Developing positive polarization.* New York: Psychosynthesis Research Foundation.

Crampton, M. (1977). *Psychosynthesis: Some key aspects of theory and practice.* Montreal: Canadian Institute of Psychosynthesis.

Cullen, J. and Russell, D. (1990). *Designing healthy organizations: An introduction to organizational Psychosynthesis.* Thousand Oaks, CA: International Association for Managerial and Organizational Psychosynthesis.

Dalton, K. (2002). *Theodore Roosevelt: A strenuous life.* New York: Alfred A Knopf.

D'Attilio, F. (2005). The restructuring of family schemes: A cognitive-behavior perspective. *Journal of Family Psychology,* 31 (1). American Psychological Association: Alexandria, VA.

deMello, A. (1978). *Sadhana, a way to God: Christian exercises in eastern form.* New York: Doubleday.

De Shazer, S. (1985). *Keys to solution in brief therapy.* New York: W.W. Norton.

Desoille, R. (1949). *Le reve eveille en psychotherapie* (the daydream in psychotherapy). Paris: Presses Universitaries de Paris.

Desoille, R. (1966). *The directed daydream.* New York: Psychosynthesis Research Foundation Issue No. 18.

Dewald, P. (1971). *Psychotherapy: A dynamic approach.* New York: Basic Books.

Eastcott, M. (1969). *The silent path: An introduction to meditation.* New York: Samuel Weiser.

Erikson, E. (1993). *Childhood and society.* New York: W.W. Norton.

Fenichel, O. (1941). *Problems of psychoanalytic technique.* Albany, N.Y.: The Psychoanalytic Quarterly.

Ferrucci, P. (1982). *What we may be.* Wellingborough, North Hamptonshire, England: Turnstone Press.

Ferrucci, P. (1990). *Inevitable grace: Breakthroughs in the lives of great men and women: guides to your self-realization.* New York: Jeremy P. Tarcher.

Firman, J. and Vargiu, J. (1977). Dimensions of growth. *Synthesis,* 3-4, 59-119. Redwood City, CA: The Synthesis Press.

Firman, J. and Russell, A. (1994). *Healing the human spirit: A Psychosynthesis view of trauma, healing, and growth.* Palo Alto, CA: Psychosynthesis Palo Alto.

Firman, J. and Gila, A. (2002). *Psychosynthesis: A psychology of spirit.* Albany, NY: State University of New York Press.

Firman, J. and Gila A. (2007). *Assagioli's seven core concepts for Psychosynthesis training.* Palo Alto. CA: Psychosynthesis Palo Alto.

Framo, J. (1970). Family of origin as a therapeutic resource for adults in marital and family therapy: You can and should go home again, *Family Process,* 15 (2), 193-210.

Framo, J. (1982). Exploration in marital and family therapy. *Selected papers of James Framo, Ph.D.* New York: Springer.

Frankl, V. (1984). *Man's search for meaning.* New York: Simon & Schuster.

Freud, S. (1916-1917). Introductory lectures on psychoanalysis. J. Strachey (Ed.), (1953). *Standard edition of the complete psychological works of Sigmund Freud,* Vols. 15 & 16. London: Hogarth Press and the Institute of Psycho-Analysis.

Freud, S. (1936). Constructions in analysis. J. Strachey (Ed.), (1953). *Standard edition of the complete psychological works of Sigmund Freud,* Vol. 23, 255-269. London: Hogarth Press.

Freud, S. (1958). *The interpretation of dreams.* New York: Basic Books.

Gerard, R. (1964). *Psychosynthesis: A psychotherapy for the whole man.* New York: Psychosynthesis Research foundation Issue No. 14.

Gilbert, D. (2006). *Stumbling on happiness.* New York: Alfred A. Knopf.

Gleick, J. (1985). *Chaos: Making a new science.* New York: Viking.

Gordon, R. (1991). *The path to the self: A Psychosynthesis primer.* Amherst, MA: Synthesis Distribution.

Gottman, J. (1994). *Why marriages succeed or fail.* New York: Simon & Schuster.

Guerin, P. J. (1976). *Family therapy: Theory and practice.* New York: Gardner Press.

Haley, J. (1977). *Uncommon therapy: The psychiatric techniques of Milton H. Erickson, M.D.* New York: W.W. Norton.

Haley, J. (1980). *Leaving home.* New York: McGraw-Hill.

Hall, C. (1966). *The meaning of dreams.* New York: McGraw-Hill.

Hall, J. A. (1983). *Jungian dream interpretation.* Toronto: Inner City Books.

Hampden-Turner, C. (1981). *Maps of the mind.* New York: Collier Books, Macmillan.

Hannah, B. (1981). *Encounters with the soul.* Boston: Sigo Press.

Hardy, J. (1996). *A psychology with a soul: Psychosynthesis in evolutionary context.* London: Woodgrange Press.

Hargrave, T. (1994). *Families and forgiveness.* New York: Brunner/Mazel.

Haronian, F. (1970). *Psychosynthesis: A psychotherapist's personal overview.* New York: Psychosynthesis Research Foundation.

Haronian, F. (1975). A psychosynthetic model of personality and its implications for psychotherapy. *Journal of Humanistic Psychology*, 15, (4), 25-53.

Haronian, F. (1977). The repression of the sublime. *Synthesis 1*, Redwood City, CA: The Synthesis Press.

Hendricks, G., and Wills, R. (1975). *The centering book: Awareness activities for children, parents, and teachers.* Englewood Cliffs, NJ: Prentice-Hall.

Hendricks, G., and Roberts, T. (1977). *The second centering book: More awareness activities for children, parents, and teachers.* New York: Prentice-Hall.

Hendrix, H. (1988). *Getting the love you want.* New York: Henry Holt.

Hillman, J. (1979). *In search: Psychology and religion.* University of Dallas, Irving, TX: Spring Publications.

Hillman, J. (1996). *The soul's code: In search of character and calling.* New York: Random House.

Houston, J. (1997). *The search for the beloved: Journeys in mythology and sacred psychology.* New York: Jeremy P. Tarcher.

Jackson, D. D. (1965). Family rules: Marital quid pro quo. *Archives of General Psychiatry*, 12, 589-594.

Jacobi, J. (1973). *The psychology of C.G. Jung.* New Haven, CT: Yale University Press.

James, William (1992). *Writings 1878-1899: Psychology, briefer course: Will to believe.* New York: Library of America, Penguin books.

Jantsch, E. and Waddington, C. (1976). *Evolution and consciousness.* Reading, MA: Addison-Wesley.

Jung, C. G. (1953). *Collected works.* New York: Pantheon Books.

Jung, C. G. (1955). *Modern man in search of a soul.* New York: Harcourt, Brace & Jovanovich.

Jung, C. G. (1961). *Memories, dreams, reflections.* New York: Random House.

Jung, C. G. (1969). *The archetypes and the collective unconscious.* Princeton, NJ: Princeton University Press.

Kaplan-Williams, S. (1988). *The Jungian-Senoi dreamwork manual: A step-by-step introduction to working with dreams.* Novato, CA: Journey Press.

Kaslow, F. (1982). Profile of the healthy family. *The Relationship*, 8 (1), 9-25.

Katherine, A. (1991). *Boundaries: Where you end and I begin.* Park Ridge, IL: Parkside Publishing.

Keeney, B. (1983). *Aesthetics of change.* New York: Guilford Press.

Kempler, W. (1981). *Experiential psychotherapy within families.* New York: Brunner/Mazel.

King, V. (1989). Psychosynthesis: A spiritual bridge. An interview by Rev. T. Harbula, *Meditation*, IV (4), p. 38, 47-51.

King, V. (1993). *Directing the drama within: An innertaining program to get your act together.* Manuscript, Santa Fe, NM: Spirit Mountain Press.

King, V. (1994). *Inner theater playbook: An interactive guide to personal change.* Santa Fe, NM: Spirit Mountain Productions.

King, V. (1998). *Being here when I need me: An inner journey.* Findhorn, Scotland: Inner Way Productions.

Kramer, J. (1985). *Family interfaces: Transgenerational patterns.* New York: Brunner/Mazel.

Kramer, S. (1988). Psychosynthesis and integrative marital and family therapy. *Readings in Psychosynthesis: Theory, process, and practice*, 2, 98-111. Toronto, ON: The Ontario Institute for Studies in Education.

Kramer, S. (1995). *Transforming the Inner and Outer Family: Humanistic and spiritual approaches to mind-body systems therapy.* New York: The Haworth Press.

L'Abate, L. and Weinstein, S. (1987). *Structured enrichment programs for couples and families.* New York: Brunner/Mazel.

LaMar, D. (2005). *Transcending Turmoil: Healing the abuse of a dysfunctional family.* Workshop and workbook by Cross Country Education, Inc. and Donna LaMar.

Lambert, C. (2007). The science of happiness. *Harvard magazine*, 109 (3), Cambridge, MA.

Legaree, T., Turner, J., and Lollis, S. (2007). Forgiveness and therapy: A critical review of conceptualizations, practices, and values found in the literature. *Journal of Marital and Family Therapy*, 33 (2), 192-212.

Lewis, J., Beavers, W., Gossett, J., and Phillips, V. (1976). *No single thread: Psychological health in family systems.* New York: Brunner/Mazel.

Linehan, M. (1993). *Skills training manual for treating borderline personality disorder.* New York: Guilford Press.

Luft, J. (1970). *Group Processes.* Palo Alto, CA: National Press Books.

Macy, J. and Brown, M. (1998). *Coming back to life: Practices to reconnect our lives, our world.* Gabriola Island, BC, Canada: New Society Publishers.

Maslow, A. H. (1968). *Toward a psychology of being.* New York: Van Nostrand.

Maslow, A. H. (1971). *The farther reaches of human nature.* New York: Viking Press.

Maturana, H. (1978). The biology of language: The epistemology of reality. G.A. Miller and E. Lenneberg (Eds.), (1978). *Psychology and biology of language and thought.* New York: Academic Press.

Maturana, H. and Varela, F. (1980). *Autopoiesis and cognition: The realization of living.* Boston: Reidel.

McBeath, B. (1984). Applications to organization development. J. Weiser and T. Yeomans (Eds.), *Psychosynthesis in the helping professions: Now and for the future.* Toronto, ON: The Ontario Institute for Studies in Education.

McBeath, B. (1988). Inquiring into organization systems: Psychosynthesis spawns a methodology. *Readings in Psychosynthesis: Theory, process, and practice,* 2, 300-307.
Toronto, ON: The Ontario Institute for Studies in Education.

McBeath, B. and Wynne, D. (1985). Integrating systems in Psychosynthesis: Applications to work with families, groups, and organizations. *Readings in Psychosynthesis: Theory, process, and practice,* 1, 172-177. Toronto, ON: The Ontario Institute for Studies in Education.

McBeath, B. and Wynne, D. (1985). Understanding organization dynamics from a Psychosynthesis perspective. *Readings in Psychosynthesis: Theory, process, & practice,* 1, 178-187. Toronto, ON: The Ontario Institute for Studies in Education.

McGoldrick, M. (1995). *You can go home again: Reconnecting with your family.* New York: W.W. Norton.

McGoldrick, M., Gerson, R., and Shellenberger, S. (1999). *Genograms: Assessment and intervention.* New York: W.W. Norton.

Miklasz, B. (July 9, 2006). Spinks earns redemption in gritty fight. St. Louis, MO: *St. Louis Post-Dispatch.*

Minuchin, S. (1974). *Families and family therapy.* Cambridge, MA: Harvard University Press.

Minuchin, S. and Fishman H. (1981). *Family therapy techniques.* Cambridge, MA: Harvard University Press.

Mitroff, I. I. (1983). *Stakeholders of the organizational mind.* San Francisco: Jossey-Bass.

Mount, F. (1982). *The subversive family.* London: Jonathan Cape.

Murdock, G. (1949). *Social structure.* New York: Macmillan.

Nichols, M. P. (1984). *Family therapy: Concepts and methods.* New York: Gardner Press.

Nouwen, H. (1988). Spirituality and the family. *Weavings,* Jan/Feb., Vol. III (1).

Nye, F. I. and Bernardo, F. M. (1981). *Emerging conceptual frameworks in family analysis.* New York: Praeger.

O'Hanlon, B. (2000). *Do one thing different: Ten simple ways to change your life.* New York: HarperCollins.

O'Hanlon, W., & Weiner-Davis, M. (1989). *In search of solutions: A new distinction in psychotherapy.* New York: W.W. Norton.

Onken, D. S. (1991). *Family synthesis: Psychosynthesis as a treatment modality in family therapy.* Unpublished doctoral dissertation, St. Louis University, St. Louis, MO.

Parfitt, W. (1990). *The Elements of Psychosynthesis.* Shaftesbury, England: Element Books.

Parfitt, W. (2003). *Psychosynthesis: The elements and beyond.* PS Avalon, Box 1865, Glastonbury, Somerset, England.

Patterson, J. M. (2002). Integrating family resilience and family stress theory. *Journal of Marriage and Family,* 64, 349-360.

Peck, M. S. (1987). *The different drum: Community making and peace.* New York: Simon & Schuster.

Perls, F. (1969). *Gestalt therapy verbatim.* Lafayette, CA: Real People Press.

Perls, F., Hefferline, R., and Goodman, P. (1951). *Gestalt therapy.* New York: Dell.

Piaget, J. (1962). *Play, dreams, and imitation in childhood.* C. Gattegna and F. Hodgson (Trans.). New York: W.W. Norton.

Platts, D. (1996). *Playful self-discovery.* Findhorn, Scotland: Findhorn Press.

Polt, W. (1980). *A generational healing experience: Connecting family systems theory and Psychosynthesis.* Paper presented at the Psychosynthesis conference, Florence, Italy.

Polt, W. (1996). *From anger to power: A Psychosynthesis approach.* Albuquerque, NM: Intermountain Publishing.

Pribam, K. (1978). What the fuss is all about. *Re-Vision,* 1, 14-18.

Progoff, I. (1975). *At a journal workshop: The basic text and guide for using the intensive journal.* New York: Dialogue House Library.

Robertson, C. (1985). Changing the context of change. *Readings in Psychosynthesis: Theory, process, and practice,* 2, 134-139.

Rogers, C. (1965). *Client-centered therapy.* Boston: Houghton Mifflin.

Rogers, C. (1978). *Carl Rogers on personal power.* New York: Delacorte.

Rossi, E. R. (1985). *Dreams and the growth of the personality: Expanding awareness in psychotherapy.* New York: Brunner/Mazel.

Rowan, J. (1991). *Subpersonalities: The people inside us.* New York: Routledge.

Russell, D. (1982). Seven basic constructs of Psychosynthesis. *Psychosynthesis Digest,* 1, (2), 67-68.

Russell, D. (1985). Psychosynthesis as a spectrum psychology. *Readings in Psychosynthesis: Theory, process, and practice,* 1, 112-133.

Sanford, J. A. (1978). *Dreams and healing: A succinct and lively interpretation of dreams.* Mahwah, NJ: Paulist Press.

Saraydarian, T. (c.2006). *Joy and healing.* Cave Creek, AZ: T.S.G. Foundation.

Satir, V. (1967). *Conjoint family therapy.* Palo Alto, CA: Science and Behavior Books.

Satir, V. (1972). *Peoplemaking.* Palo Alto, CA: Science and Behavior Books.

Satir, V. (1982). The therapist and family therapy: Process model. A. Horne and M. Ohlsen (Eds.), *Family counseling and therapy.* Itasca, IL: F.E. Peacock.

Satir, V. and Baldwin, M. (1983). *Satir step by step: A guide to creating change in families.* Palo Alto, CA: Science and Behavior Books.

Satir, V., Stachowiak, J, and Taschman, H. (1977). *Helping families to change.* New York: Aronson.

Sawin, M. M. (1979). *Family enrichment with family clusters.* Valley Forge, PA: Judson Press.

Scharff, D. E. and Scharff, J. S. (1987). *Object relations family therapy.* Northvale, NJ: Jason Aronson.

Schultz, S. J. (1984) *Family systems therapy: An integration.* New York: Jason Aronson.

Seligman, M. (1990). *Learned Optimism.* New York: Random House.

Seligman, M. (1995). *The optimistic child.* Boston: Houghton Mifflin.

Seligman, M. (2002). *Authentic happiness: Using the new positive psychology to realize your potential for lasting fulfillment.* New York: Free Press.

Selvini, M. (Ed.). (1988). *The work of Mara Selvini Papazzoli.* Northvale, NJ: Jason Aronson.

Siegel, B. (1995). Love: The work of the soul. R. Carlson and B. Shields (Eds.), *Healers on healing.* Los Angeles, CA: Jeremy P. Tarcher, 39-44.

Singer, J. (1973). *Boundaries of the soul: The practice of Jung's psychology.* Garden city, NJ: Anchor Books, Doubleday.

Sliker, G. (1992). *Multiple Mind: Healing the split in psyche and world.* Boston, MA: Shambala.

Stahl, C. (1977). *Opening to God: Guided imagery meditation on Scripture.* Nashville, TN: Upper Room.

Smith, D. (1982). Trends in counseling and psychotherapy. *American Psychologist,* 37, (7), 802-809.

Stauffer, E. R. (1987). *Unconditional love and forgiveness.* Diamond Springs, CA: Triangle Publishers.

Steward, J. (1953). *Theory of culture change.* Urbana, IL: University of Illinois Press.

Swami Ajaya (1983). *Psychotherapy east and west: A unifying paradigm.* Honesdale, PA: The Himalayan International Institute of Yoga Science and Philosophy of the USA.

Szent-Gyoergyi, A. (1977) Drive in living matter to perfect itself. *Synthesis 1.* Redwood City, CA: Synthesis Press.

Taylor, G. (1968). *The essentials of Psychosynthesis.* New York: Psychosynthesis Research Foundation.

Taylor, G. and Crampton, M. (1968). *Approaches to the Self: The "Who am I" techniques in psychotherapy.* New York: Psychosynthesis Research Foundation.

Taylor, J. (1983). *DreamWork: Techniques for discovering the creative power in dreams.* New York: Paulist Press.

The new Oxford annotated Bible (1991). Metzger, B. and Murphy, R. (Eds.). New York, Oxford University Press.

Vaillant, G. (1995). *Adaptation to life.* Cambridge, MA: Harvard University Press.

Val-Essen, I. (1997). *Bring out the best in your child and yourself.* Culver City, CA: Quality Parenting.

Vargiu, J. (1971). *Global education and Psychosynthesis.* New York: Psychosynthesis Research Foundation.

Vargiu, J. (1977). Subpersonalities. *Synthesis* 1. Redwood City, CA: Synthesis Press, 52-90.

Vargiu, J. and Vargiu S. (1977). Personal growth and the family: A conversation with Virginia Satir. *Synthesis* 3-4. Redwood City, CA: Synthesis Press, 172-193.

Von Franz, M. (1970). *Interpretations of fairy tales.* Dallas, TX: Spring Publications.

Wachtel, E. and Wachtel, P. (1986). *Family dynamics in individual psychotherapy. A guide to clinical strategies.* New York: Guilford Press.

Walsh, F. (1991). Promoting healthy functioning in divorced and remarried families. A. Gurman and D. Kniskern (Eds.), *Handbook of family therapy.* New York: Brunner/Mazel.

Walsh, F. (1993). Conceptualization of normal family processes. F. Walsh (Ed.), *Normal Family Processes.* New York: Guilford Press.

Walsh, F. (1998). *Strengthening family resilience.* New York: Guilford Press.

Walsh, F. (2003). *Normal family processes: Growing diversity and complexity.* New York: Guilford Press.

Watkins, J., and Watkins, H. (1997). *Ego states: Theory and therapy.* New York: W.W. Norton.

Watzlawick, P., Weakland, J., and Fisch, R. (1974). *Change: Principles of problem resolution.* New York: W.W. Norton.

Whitaker, C. A. (1976). A family is a four-dimensional relationship. P. Guerin (Ed.), *Family therapy: Theory and practice.* New York: Gardner Press.

Whitaker, C. and Keith, D. (1981). Symbolic-experiential family therapy. A. Gurman and D. Kniskern (Eds.), *Handbook of family therapy.* New York: Brunner/Mazel.

Whitaker, C., Rose, J., Geiser, F., and Johnson, N. (1982). The role of silence in brief psychotherapy. J. Neill and D. Kniskern (Eds.), *From psyche to system.* New York: Guilford Press.

White, R. and Gilliland, R. (1975). *Elements of psychopathology: The mechanism of defense.* New York: Harcourt, Brace & Jovanovich.

Whitfield, C. (1989). *Healing the child within.* Deerfield Beach, FL: Health Communications.

Whitmore, D. (1986). *Psychosynthesis in education.* Rochester, VT: Destiny Books.

Wilber, K. (1977). *The spectrum of consciousness.* Wheaton, IL: The Theosophical Publishing House.

Wilber, K. (1985). *No boundary: Eastern and western approaches to spiritual growth.* Boston: Shambhala.

Wolff, C. (1734). *Rational psychology.* M. Bigge, and M. Hunt, *Psychological foundations of education.* New York: Harper & Row.

Wolin, S. and Bennett, L. (1984). Family Rituals. *Family Process,* 12 (3), 401-420.

Wolin, S. and Wolin, S. (1993). *The resilient self: How survivors of troubled families rise above adversity.* New York: Villard.

Wuerffel, J. Defrain, J., and Stinnett, N. (1990). How strong families use humor. *Family perspective,* 24, 129-142.

Wynne, L., Ryckoff, I., Day, J. and Hirsch, S., (1958). Pseudomutuality in the family relations of schizophrenics. *Psychiatry*, 21, 205-220.

Yalom, I (1970). *The theory and practice of group psychotherapy.* New York: Basic Books.

Yeomans, T. (1984). Psychosynthesis in the helping professions. J. Weiser and T. Yeomans (Eds.), *Psychosynthesis in the helping professions: Now and for the future.* Toronto, ON: Ontario Institute for Studies in Education.

Yeomans, T. (1990). *Psychosynthesis practice: Psychosynthesis exercises for personal and spiritual growth.* vol. I. San Jose, CA: Psychosynthesis Distribution.

Yeomans, T. (1996). *The Corona process: Group work in a spiritual context.* Concord, MA: Concord Institute Publications.

Yeomans, T. (1999). *Soul on earth: Readings in spiritual psychology.* Concord, MA: The Concord Institute.

Young, P., (1988). Family of origin: Land of opportunity for Psychosynthesis. *Readings in Psychosynthesis: Theory, process, and practice, 2, 6-14.* Toronto, ON: Ontario Institute for Studies in Education.

Zukav, G. (1990). *The seat of the soul.* New York: Simon & Schuster.

Made in the USA
Monee, IL
02 January 2023